ARTIFICIAL INTELLIGENCE, BLOCKCHAIN & QUANTUM COMPUTING

DAVID SANDUA

"Blockchain, Artificial Intelligence and Quantum Computing are the foundations of the fourth industrial revolution."

Technology Economist

INDEX

INTRODUCTION

Artificial Intelligence (AI), blockchain, and quantum computer science are three emerging technology that are transforming various aspects of our life. This technology have the potential to revolutionize industry, improve efficiency, and solve complex problem. In recent old age, there has been a significant addition in inquiry and evolution in this area, leading to numerous promotion and discovery. AI, blockchain, and quantum computer science are interconnected in many shipways, with each engineering complementing and enabling the others. This try aims to explore the current province and future prospect of this technology, their wallop on different sector, and the challenge they pose. AI has been a subject of involvement and inquiry for several decades, but the recent promotion in computing powerless and information handiness have propelled its evolution to new high. AI mention to the creative activity and execution of intelligent machine that can mimic human cognitive procedure such as acquisition, logical thinking, and problem-solving. Machine acquisition, a subfield of AI, focuses on developing algorithms that allow machine to learn from information and improve their public presentation without explicit scheduling. This engineering has found application in area like health care, finance, and transportation system, revolutionizing the manner undertaking are performed and enabling new possibility. AI has the potential to enhance efficiency, truth, and productiveness across various industry, leading to cost nest egg and increased fight. Blockchain, on the other minus, is a decentralized and distributed

Leger engineering that enables to procure and transparent interchange of digital asset without the demand for mediator. It was initially popularized by cryptocurrencies like Bitcoin, but its potential range far beyond digital currency. The key feature of blockchain, including immutableness, transparency, and protection, make it suitable for a wide scope of application, such as provision concatenation direction, health care phonograph record direction, and financial minutes. By eliminating the demand for mediator and providing a tamper-resistant phonograph record of minutes, blockchain can reduce cost, streamline procedure, and enhance reliance among participant. The acceptance of blockchain engineering has been growing steadily, with numerous industry exploring its potential and developing innovative usage case. Quantum computer science is a battlefield that combines principle from natural philosophy, math, and computing machine scientific discipline to develop powerful computer that can perform complex calculation much faster than classical computer. Unlike classical computer that use spot to store and manipulate info, quantum computer use quantum spot, or qubits, which can exist in multiple state simultaneously. These belonging allows quantum computer to perform calculation at an exponential scale of measurement, solving problem that are currently infeasible with conventional computing system. Quantum computer science has the potential to revolutionize fields such as cryptanalysis, optimization, dose find, and material scientific discipline. Quantum computer are still in the early phase of evolution, and many technical challenge need to be overcome before they become commercially viable. Despite their potential benefit, AI, blockchain, and quantum computer science also pose significant challenge. Ethical consideration, such as occupation supplanting and information privateers, originate with the increasing acceptance of AI system. Blockchain faces scalability and interoperability issue, as well as regulatory and legal challenge. Quantum computing faces multiple technical challenge, including the demand for quantum mistake rectification, qubit staleness, and improved control condition mechanism. The integrating of this technology is not straightforward, as AI algorithm can be computationally intensive, while quantum computing trust on the delicate use of quantum state, which can be easily disrupted. To fully harness the potentiality of AI, blockchain, and quantum computer science, interdisciplinary coaction and ongoing inquiry are required. In decision, AI, blockchain, and quantum computer science are emerging technology that have the potentiality to transform industry and solve complex problem. They offer new possibility and improved efficiency, but they also present challenge that need to be addressed. The integrating of this technology can lead to exciting promotion and application that were previously unimaginable. As the inquiry and evolution in this area continue to progress, it is essential to explore their potential wallop, computer address challenge, and develop model that ensure their responsible and ethical usage. Only through collaborative attempt can we fully unlock the transformative powerless of AI, blockchain, and quantum computer science.

DEFINITION OF ARTIFICIAL INTELLIGENCE

AI is a condition used to describe the power of machine or computing machine system to simulate human-like intelligence service. It encompasses a scope of technology and technique that aim to enable machine to perform undertaking that typically require human intelligence service, such as acquisition, problem-solving, percent, and logical thinking. The end of AI is to create intelligent machine that can replicate or enhance human decision-making, apprehension, and problem-solving capability. AI is a very broad battlefield, with multiple subfields, including simple machine acquisition, natural linguistic communication process, computing machine sight, robotics, and expert system, among others. Machine acquisition is a key constituent of AI, as it allows machine to learn from and make prediction or decision based on large sum of information. This involves the evolution of algorithm and model that can analyze and interpret information, place form, and make decision or prediction with minimal human intercession. Machine acquisition can be divided into two main type : supervised acquisition and unsupervised acquisition. Supervised learning involve training a simple machine to recognize form or make prediction based on labeled information, in which the desire end product is known. Unsupervised acquisition, on the other minus, involves training a simple machine to identify form or make prediction based on unlabeled information, without a known desired end product. Natural linguistic communication process (natural language processing) is another important subfield of AI, which focuses on enabling machine to understand, interpret, and generate human linguistic communication. Natural language processing involves the evolution of algorithm and model that can process, analyze, and generate natural linguistic communication textual matter or address. This allows machine to interact and communicate with world in a more natural and intuitive manner. Natural language processing has many applications, including linguistic communication interlingual rendition, opinion analytic thinking, chatbots, virtual assistant, and vocalization acknowledgment. Computer sight is another subfield of AI that aims to enable machine to analyze, interpret, and understand visual information. This involves developing algorithm and model that can process and analyze image or video, identify object or form, and extract meaningful info from visual information. Computer sight has numerous application, including facial acknowledgment, object sensing, autonomous vehicle, and medical mental image analytic thinking. Robotics is another subfield of AI that combines component of mechanical technology, electrical technology, and computing machine scientific discipline to design, develop, and deploy automaton. Automaton are autonomous machine that can perform undertaking with minimal human intercession. They can be used in various application, including fabrication, health care, geographic expedition, and defense. AI plays a crucial function in robotics, as it enables machine to perceive and interpret their environs, program and execute action, and learn from their experience. Expert system are another subfield of AI that aims to create computing machine system that can emulate the decision-making and problem-solving capability of human expert in specific sphere. This system are designed to integrate and apply large sum of cognition and expertness in order of magnitude to assist world in making complex decision or solving difficult problem. Expert system can be used in a wide scope of sphere, including medical specialty, jurisprudence, finance, and technology. In decision, AI encompasses a scope of technology and technique that aim to enable machine to simulate human-like intelligence service. It involves the evolution of algorithm and model that can analyze and interpret information, realize and bring forth human linguistic communication, procedure and analyze visual information, and emulate human decision-making and problem-solving capability. AI has numerous application and subfields, including simple machine acquisition, natural linguistic communication process, computing machine sight, robotics, and expert system. The end of AI is to create intelligent machine that can replicate or enhance human decision-making, apprehension, and problem-solving capability. As AI continues to advance, it has the potential to revolutionize various industry and transform the manner we live and piece of work.

DEFINITION OF BLOCKCHAIN

Blockchain is a revolutionary engineering that has gained significant attending in recent old age. It is often hailed as a game-changer in various sectors, including finance, provision concatenation direction, health care, and beyond. In kernel, blockchain can be defined as a decentralized and distributed Leger that shop information in a serial of block, which are linked together using cryptographic algorithm. Each city block contains a unique identifier, a timestamp, and a phonograph record of minutes or information. The associate between block is achieved through a digital touch, which ensures the unity and immutableness of the information stored within the blockchain. This means that once a city block is added to the blockchain, it cannot be altered or manipulated, providing a high degree of protection and reliance. The decentralized nature of blockchain eliminates the demand for mediator, such as Banks or other financial institution, as minutes can be directly executed between party involved. This not only reduces cost but also increases efficiency and transparency in the procedure. To validate and verify the info stored on the blockchain, a consensus chemical mechanism is employed. This chemical mechanism ensures that all participant in the web hold on the cogency of the information without the demand for a central authorization. One of the most common consensus mechanism is the proof-of-work (prisoner of war), which requires participant, known as miner, to solve complex mathematical problem to add new block to the blockchain. This procedure not only secures the web but also incentivizes participant

17

to contribute their computing powerless and resource. Another consensus chemical mechanism that has gained popularity is the proof-of-stake (polonium), which selects the validator of a new city block based on their interest or possession of the cryptocurrency associated with the blockchain. As a consequence, the polonium chemical mechanism consumes significantly less free energy compared to prisoner of war, making it more environmentally friendly. It is worth mentioning that blockchain is not limited to financial minutes or cryptocurrency application. Its potential widen to various industry, where reliance, protection, and transparency are essential. For case, provision concatenation direction could greatly benefit from blockchain engineering by providing a crystalline and immutable phonograph record of every dealing or transportation of good. This would enable business and consumer to trace the beginning and genuineness of merchandise, thus combating counterfeiting and ensuring the ethical source of material. Healthcare organization could leverage blockchain to securely store and portion affected role record, ensuring information privateers while enabling faster and more accurate diagnosis. The immense potentiality of blockchain has led to the outgrowth of numerous start-ups, inquiry enterprise, and speculation investing in this battlefield. Developer and pioneer are continuously exploring new usage case and application of this engineering to disrupt traditional system and procedure. It is crucial to acknowledge the challenge and restriction that blockchain faces. Firstly, scalability remains a persistent number, especially with public blockchains. As the figure of minutes and participant in the web addition, the process clip and monetary value also grow, making it less practical for high-volume application. This has led to the evolution of solution such as off-chain minutes, side-chains, and layer-two protocol to address scalability concern. Secondly, interoperability between different blockchains is another dispute that needs to be overcome. As the figure of blockchain network and protocol continues to grow, it becomes essential to establish standard and protocol for seamless communicating and information transportation between this network. The regulatory and legal model surrounding blockchain engineering are still evolving. The decentralized nature of blockchain airs unique challenge for government and regulatory body in footing of information privateers, personal identity confirmation, and enforcement of Torah. It is essential to strike a proportion between fostering invention and ensuring conformity and protection. In decision, the definition of blockchain encompasses a decentralized and distributed Leger, utilizing cryptographic algorithm, digital signature, and consensus mechanism to store and verify information in a procured and transparent mode. Its potential application span across various industry, providing solution to long-standing challenge related to trust, protection, and efficiency. Despite its ballyhoo and potentiality, blockchain is not without its restriction and challenge. Scalability, interoperability, and regulatory model are area that require continuous inquiry and evolution to fully unleash the potentiality of blockchain engineering. Nonetheless, the growing involvement, investing, and collaboration in this battlefield indicate that blockchain is poised to revolutionize numerous sector and shape the hereafter of our digital universe.

DEFINITION OF QUANTUM COMPUTING

Quantum computer science is a subdivision of computing machine scientific discipline that utilizes the principle of quantum mechanism to perform complex calculation at an unprecedented velocity and efficiency. Unlike classical computer, which use spot to store and process info, quantum computer employ quantum spot, or qubits, which can exist in multiple state simultaneously. This inherent belongings of qubits is known as principle of superposition and allows quantum computer to evaluate many possible solutions at once, thereby greatly accelerating the computational procedure. In order of magnitude to fully grasp the potentiality of quantum computer science, it is crucial to understand the conception of principle of superposition. Unlike classical spot, which can only represent either a 0 or a 1, qubits can simultaneously represent both 0 and This is due to the fact that qubits exist in a province that is a combining of 0 and 1, known as a quantum principle of superposition province. For case, a qubit can exist in a principle of superposition province that is 50 % 0 and 50 % 1, or any other combining of probability. This unique belongings let quantum computer to process multiple calculation simultaneously, exponentially increasing their computational powerless. In add-on to principle of superposition, another fundamental rule of quantum computer science is entanglement. Web is a phenomenon that occurs when two or more qubits become connected in such a manner that the province of one qubit is dependent on the province of another, regardless of the length between them. This means that the province of one qubit cannot be described independently of its entangled spouse, regardless of whether they are in close propinquity or at opposite end of the existence. The conception of web is critical for quantum computer science as it enables the synchronize and core relativity of qubits, allowing for the executing of complex calculation that are beyond the capability of classical computer. The potential application of quantum computing span multiple discipline, including cryptanalysis, optimization, dose find, and artificial intelligence service. One of the most significant area where quantum computer science can have a profound wallop is cryptanalysis. With the coming of quantum computer, the current cryptanalytic technique that protect sensitive info may become vulnerable to attack. Quantum computer could potentially crack encoding code with easiness, rendering traditional form of information protection disused. Quantum cryptanalysis, which utilizes the principle of quantum mechanism to ensure secure communicating, may offer an answer to this job. By leveraging the property of quantum web and principle of superposition, quantum cryptanalysis provides a manner to transmit info in a mode that cannot be intercepted or decoded by malicious actor. Another country where quantum computing holds tremendous hope is optimization. Many real-world problem are inherently complex and require the geographic expedition of an astronomical figure of possibility. Classical computer struggle to solve such problem due to their sequential process nature, but quantum computer, with their power to evaluate multiple possibility simultaneously, can potentially provide optimal solution efficiently. This has significant deduction in fields such as provision concatenation direction, programming, and logistics, where the power to make optimal decision can greatly enhance efficiency and effectivity. Further, quantum computer science could revolutionize the battlefield of dose find. The procedure of developing new medicine is notoriously time-consuming and expensive, often involving the rating of countless chemical compound to identify potential dose campaigner. By leveraging the parallel process paleness of quantum computer, research worker can significantly accelerate the find procedure by simulating the behavior of molecule and predicting their pharmacological property. This would enable the designation of promising dose campaigner in a divide of the clip and resource required by classical method. Quantum computer science has the potential to revolutionize artificial intelligence service. Traditional simple machine acquisition algorithm require large sum of computational powerless to procedure and analyze complex datasets. Quantum computer, with their huge process capability, can potentially speed up the preparation and executing of simple machine acquisition model, enabling the evolution of more sophisticated and accurate AI system. This integrating of quantum computer science and AI could lead to breakthroughs in various spheres, including mental image acknowledgment, natural linguistic communication process, and autonomous vehicle. In decision, quantum computer science is a rapidly developing battlefield that has the potential to revolutionize various industry and scientific discipline. By harnessing the principle of superposition and web, quantum computer offer unparalleled computational powerless that could enable groundbreaking progress in cryptanalysis, optimization, dose find, and artificial intelligence service.

As inquiry and evolution go on, it is crucial to explore the ethical, privateers, and protection deduction of quantum computer science, ensuring the responsible and beneficial use of this powerful engineering.

IMPORTANCE OF THESE TECHNOLOGIES

The grandness of this technology cannot be overstated. AI service, blockchain, and quantum computing have the potential to revolutionize various industry and sector in unimaginable slipway. First and foremost, artificial intelligence service has already begun to shape our life in numerous slipway, from virtual assistant like Siri and Alexa to autonomous vehicle. AI has the power to streamline procedure, improve productiveness, and enhance decision-making. For case, in the health care sphere, AI algorithm can analyze large datasets to predict disease outbreak, identify form in affected role information, and aid in the diagnosing and intervention of disease. This has the potential to revolutionize healthcare bringing and improve affected role result. Similarly, in the financial manufacture, AI-powered algorithm can detect fraudulent activity, predict marketplace tendency, and automate various undertaking, thereby increasing efficiency and reducing cost. AI also holds great hope in the battlefield of instruction, where it can personalize learning experience for student, accommodate to their individual need, and provide instant feedback. This can lead to a more engaging and effective educational see for learner of all age. In add-on to artificial intelligence service, blockchain engineering has gained significant attending in recent old age. Blockchain, essentially a decentralized Leger, has the potential to revolutionize various industry, particularly those that involve minutes and information storehouse. One of the key benefit of blockchain is its power to provide transparency and protection. By decentralizing the storehouse and confirmation of information, blockchain eliminates the demand for mediator, such as Banks or authorities agency. This can lead to cost nest egg, increased efficiency, and reduced opportunity of imposter. For case, in the financial sphere, blockchain engineering can enable faster, cheaper, and more secure cross-border minutes. It can also be applied to supply concatenation direction, where it can track the motion of good and verify their genuineness, thereby mitigating the hazard of counterfeiting. Blockchain can enhance information protection and privateers by providing person with greater control condition over their personal info. This has deduction in various sectors, including health care, where affected role information can be securely stored and accessed by authorized person only. Blockchain engineering has the potential to disrupt traditional concern model and create new opportunity for invention. Quantum computer science is a rapidly emerging battlefield that promises to dramatically enhance computing powerless and solve complex problem that are currently beyond the capability of classical computer. Unlike classical computer that use spot to store info, quantum computer utilize quantum spot or qubits, which can exist in both 0 and 1 state simultaneously. These belongings, known as principle of superposition, allow quantum computer to perform massive analogue calculation and solve problem much faster than classical computer. Quantum computer science has the potential to revolutionize fields such as cryptanalysis, optimization, and dose find. For case, quantum computer can break current encoding algorithm, posing both a dispute and a chance for cybersecurity. They can optimize complex logistical trading operations, such as path preparation or resourcefulness allotment, leading to increased efficiency and monetary value nest egg. In the battlefield of dose find, quantum computer can simulate the behavior of molecule and accelerate the evolution of new drug. This can have a significant wallop on health care by enabling the find of more effective treatment for various disease. While quantum computer science is still in its early phase of evolution, it holds immense hope for the hereafter. In decision, the grandness of artificial intelligence service, blockchain, and quantum computing cannot be ignored. This technology have the potential to revolutionize various sector and industry, ranging from health care and finance to instruction and cybersecurity. AI service can improve decision-making, heighten productiveness, and personalize learning experience. Blockchain engineering can provide transparency, protection, and efficiency in minutes, information storehouse, and provision concatenation direction. Quantum computing can exponentially enhance computing powerless and solve complex problem that are beyond the capability of classical computer. As this technology continue to advance, it is essential for person, organization, and government to understand their potential and harness them effectively to drive invention and create a better hereafter.

PURPOSE OF THE ESSAY

The intent of this try is to explore the possibility and deduction of AI, blockchain engineering, and quantum computer science. AI, in its various forms, has already begun to revolutionize numerous industry and aspect of daily living. From vocalization assistant like Siri and Alexa to self-driving car and personalized recommendation on streaming platform, AI has quickly become a ubiquitous front. Through the analytic thinking of existing inquiry and instance survey, this try aims to delve into the potential hereafter promotion that AI can bring to fields such as health care, finance, and transportation system. The try will examine the ethical consideration surrounding the usage of AI and the grandness of ensuring that this technology are developed and utilized responsibly. This try seeks to provide an overview of blockchain engineering and its function in transforming traditional system of record-keeping and dealing confirmation. As a decentralized and transparent Leger engineering, blockchain has the potential to greatly impact sector such as finance, provision concatenation direction, and voting system. By analyzing real-life example and exploring the challenge and opportunity that blockchain present, this try aims to highlight the potential benefit of this engineering and its possible application in various industry. This try will explore the emerging battlefield of quantum computer science and its potential to revolutionize computing powerless and problem-solving capability. Unlike classical computer science, which relies on spot, quantum computing utilizes quantum spot, or qubits, which can exist in a principle of superposition of state. This unique belongings let quantum computer to perform calculation and solve complex problem exponentially faster than classical computer. Through a scrutiny of current inquiry and development, this try will discuss the potential application of quantum computing in fields such as cryptanalysis, dose find, and optimization. The intent of this try is to provide an overview of the promotion and possibility of AI, blockchain engineering, and quantum computer science. By exploring the existing inquiry and real-life example, this try aims to shed visible light on the potential benefit and challenges this technology present. The try seeks to engage in a treatment about the ethical consideration surrounding the usage of AI, the transformative powerless of blockchain, and the potentiality of quantum computing to revolutionize computing as we know it. By examining these subject, this try aims to contribute to the conversation surrounding the hereafter of engineering and its deduction for various industry and club as a unit. In decision, the intent of this try is to provide a comprehensive overview of the possibility and deduction of artificial intelligence service, blockchain engineering, and quantum computer science. By examining existing inquiry and real-world example, this try seeks to shed visible light on the potential benefit and challenges this technology present. The try aims to engage in a treatment about the ethical consideration surrounding the usage of AI, the transformative powerless of blockchain, and the potentiality of quantum computing to revolutionize computing as we know it. Through the geographic expedition of these subject, this try contributes to the ongoing conversation surrounding the hereafter of engineering and its wallop on club.

Despite the numerous promotion in scientific discipline and engineering, the universe is still at the leaflet of a new epoch of invention and transmutation. Three emerging technology, artificial intelligence service, blockchain, and quantum computer science, have the potential to reshape industry, revolutionize procedure, and redefine the manner we live and piece of work. This technology are not only interconnected, but they also complement each other, creating a synergism that opens up endless possibility for the hereafter. Artificial AI is the computer simulation of human intelligence service in machine that are programmed to think, learn, and problem-solve like world. AI has already made significant pace in various sectors such as health care, finance, and transportation system, but its full potentiality is yet to be realized. One country where AI has shown immense hope is in the battlefield of medical specialty. In the coming old age, AI-powered system can analyze massive sum of medical information and aid in diagnosis, accelerating the procedure and improving truth. AI has the potentiality to improve affected role attention by predicting disease and identifying potential hazard, thereby enabling proactive measure to be taken. In the financial sphere, AI algorithm can analyze vast sum of information to identify form and tendency, enabling more effective hazard direction and imposter sensing. AI-powered chatbots can enhance client religious service by providing round-the-clock aid, resolving question, and even personalizing experience. As AI continues to evolve, it will undoubtedly transform industry and heighten productiveness in slipway previously unimaginable. Another engineering that has garnered significant attending is blockchain, a distributed Leger engineering that provides a procured and transparent manner of transcription and verifying minutes. Initially popularized by Bitcoin, blockchain has since transcended its cryptocurrency root and is now being explored for numerous application in various sectors. One country where blockchain can have a transformative wallop is supply concatenation direction. By utilizing blockchain engineering, company can ensure the unity and transparency of their provision irons, allowing for seamless traceability and the riddance of imposter or forge. Blockchain can also streamline the cumbrous processes involved in real land minutes, reducing paperwork, minimizing imposter, and expediting the overall procedure. Blockchain can revolutionize the health care manufacture by securely storing and sharing affected role information, facilitating interoperability, and enhancing privateers. The decentralization provided by blockchain engineering offer immense potential in footing of democratizing info and empower person. As this engineering matures and becomes more widely adopted, it will undoubtedly disrupt traditional concern model and create new avenue for invention. One of the most anticipated and radical technology on the apparent horizon is quantum computing. Unlike classical computer, which use spot to process info as either a 0 or 1, quantum computer use quantum spot or qubits, which can exist simultaneously in multiple state. This unique belongings of qubits enable quantum computer to perform certain calculation exponentially faster than classical computer. Quantum computing holds enormous potentiality for solving complex problem that are currently intractable. For illustration, in the battlefield of dose find, quantum computer can rapidly analyze the vast figure of possible molecular interaction and predict the most effective compound

32

to develop as potential drug. Quantum computer can revolutionize cryptanalysis by rendering current encoding method obsolete. The power of quantum computer to factor large Numbers in a divide of the clip it takes classical computer has the potential to disrupt cybersecurity and necessitate the evolution of new encoding algorithm. Despite its immense potentiality, quantum computer science is still in its babyhood, and many technical challenge need to be overcome before its widespread acceptance. The advancement made so far in this battlefield is encouraging, and the wallop of quantum computing on various industry is likely to be revolutionary. The convergence of these three technology is what makes this epoch of invention so exciting and promise. AI, blockchain, and quantum computer science are not standalone technology but rather complementary and interconnected. For case, AI can enhance the information analytic thinking capability of blockchain by extracting penetration and form from vast sum of information, while blockchain can provide the protection and transparency required for handling sensitive AI-generated end product. Similarly, quantum computing can exponentially accelerate the velocity at which AI algorithm procedure information, enabling rapid promotion in AI-powered system. The combining of this technology has the potential to unlock new frontier of invention and Usher in a new epoch of transformative alteration. In decision, the convergence of artificial intelligence service, blockchain, and quantum computer science is poised to reshape industry, redefine procedure, and revolutionize the manner we live and piece of work. Each of these technology holds immense hope individually, but it is their interplay and synergism that amplify their potential. As this technology continue to evolve and mature, it is crucial for policymakers, business, and club at large to understand their deduction, computer address challenge, and harness their transformative powerless for the welfare of all. The hereafter is uncertain, but one matter is for certain – the intersection point of AI, blockchain, and quantum computer science will shape the universe we live in for old age to come.

II. ARTIFICIAL INTELLIGENCE

AI is a rapidly developing battlefield with the potential to revolutionize various aspects of our life. AI mention to the evolution of computing machine system that are capable of performing undertaking that typically require human intelligence service, such as acquisition, problem-solving, and decision-making. The battlefield of AI has witnessed significant promotion in recent old age, thanks to the handiness of vast sum of information and the increasing computational powerless of machine. One of the key area where AI has made a remarkable wallop is in health care. AI-powered system have the potentiality to streamline and improve various procedure in the health care manufacture. For case, simple machine learning algorithm can analyze large sum of medical information and identify form that human doctor may miss. This can help in more accurate diagnosis and personalized intervention plan. AI-powered automaton can assist in performing operating room with greater preciseness, reducing the hazard of human mistake. AI-based chatbots are being used to provide basic health care info to patient, thereby reducing the stress on health care supplier. Another country where AI is making significant promotion is in the kingdom of self-driving car. Company like tesla and Google are investing heavily in developing autonomous vehicle that can navigate the roadstead without human intercession. These vehicle use AI algorithm to interpret information from various detectors, such as camera and radar, to make real-time decision. The potential wallop of self-driving car is enormous, as they have the potential to reduce accident and dealings over-crowding, as well as addition fire efficiency. There are still several challenges that need to be overcome before self-driving car can become mainstream. Safety concern, ethical dilemma, and regulatory issue are at the head of this challenge. AI is also being applied in the battlefield of finance and investing. Machine learning algorithm can analyze vast sum of financial information and predict marketplace tendency with a high grade of truth. This can help investor make informed decision and optimize their investing portfolio. AI-based trade algorithm can execute trade at extremely high speed, minimizing dealing cost and increasing efficiency. There are concern regarding the potentiality of AI to exacerbate marketplace unpredictability and make unforeseen financial hazard. The trust on algorithm and the deficiency of human intercession may lead to unintended consequence and marketplace use. AI is being used to enhance the efficiency and effectivity of client religious service. Many companies are employing chatbots to handle client question and provide aid. These chatbots use natural linguistic communication process algorithm to understand and respond to client request. They can provide instant response and are available 24/7, eliminating the demand for customer to wait for human aid. AI-powered virtual assistant, such as apple's Siri or amazon's Alexa, are becoming increasingly popular for their power to perform a wide scope of undertaking, from setting reminder to controlling smart place device. There are concern about the potential deprivation of occupation in client religious service as more company adopt AI-based solution. AI is being utilized in the battlefield of instruction to provide personalized and adaptive acquisition experience. Intelligent tutoring system can analyze the acquisition form of student and tailor educational message accordingly. This can help student grasp difficult concept more easily and at their own gait. AI-based grading system can automate the scaling procedure, reducing the load on teacher and providing faster feedback to student. There are concern about the potentiality of AI to replace human teacher and the deficiency of emotional intelligence service in AI system. In decision, artificial intelligence service has the potential to revolutionize various sectors, from health care to finance to client religious service to instruction. The promotion in AI engineering have opened up new possibility for improving efficiency, truth, and mechanization. There are several challenge and concern that need to be addressed, such as refuge, ethical motive, occupation supplanting, and regulatory issue. It is crucial to strike a proportion between harnessing the potentiality of AI and ensuring that it is developed and deployed responsibly, with the best interest of club in head.

OVERVIEW OF AI

Overview of AI artificial intelligence is a subdivision of computing machine scientific discipline that focuses on the evolution of intelligent system capable of performing undertaking that typically require human intelligence service. The conception of AI can be traced back to antediluvian multiplication, with mythological narrative and folklore often depicting machine with human-like intelligence service. The battlefield of AI as we know it nowadays began to take form in the mid-20th hundred. The condition AI was coined by toilet Mary McCarthy, the male parent of AI, in 1956. Mary McCarthy, along with a grouping of research worker at Dartmouth College, organized the Dartmouth College conference, which is widely considered to be the place of birth of AI. AI can be categorized into two main type : contract AI and general AI. Narrow AI, also known as weak AI, refers to system that are designed to perform specific undertaking and operate within a limited sphere. Example of narrow AI include vocalization assistant like Siri, self-driving car, and algorithms that recommend movie or merchandise based on our preference. This system rely on simple machine acquisition algorithm, which enable them to learn and improve over clip through vulnerability to large sum of information. On the other minus, general AI, or strong AI, refers to system that possess the power to understand, learn, and apply cognition across different sphere similar to human intelligence service. General AI aims to replicate human knowledge and reasoning ability. Despite significant advancement in the battlefield of AI, achieving general AI still remains a grand dispute. Research worker are working on developing algorithm and architectures that can enable machine to think, ground, and solve problem in a mode similar to world. The key component of AI include simple machine acquisition, natural linguistic communication process (natural language processing), computing machine sight, and robotics. Machine acquisition is a subset of AI that focuses on algorithm and statistical model that enable machine to learn from and make prediction or decision based on information. The handiness of large datasets and powerful computing resource has revolutionized the battlefield of simple machine acquisition, leading to breakthroughs in various application such as mental image acknowledgment and linguistic communication interlingual rendition. Natural language processing, another important constituent of AI, deal with the fundamental interaction between computer and human linguistic communication. Natural language processing technique allow computer to understand, interpret, and generate human linguistic communication, enabling technology such as address acknowledgment, simple machine interlingual rendition, and chatbots. Computer sight, on the other minus, is concerned with the reading of visual info by machine. Computer sight algorithm can analyze and extract meaningful info from image and video, opening up possibility in area like autonomous drive, medical imagination, and surveillance. Robotics, the final constituent of AI, deal with the evolution and practical application of automaton and intelligent machine. Automaton can be equipped with AI capability to perform physical undertaking in an assortment of environment. From autonomous drone to industrial automation, AI-powered machine are being increasingly used in industry to automate procedure, heighten productiveness, and perform undertaking that are too dangerous or tedious for world. The integrating of AI and robotics is also giving ascent to the evolution of social automaton that can interact with world, providing company, aid, and amusement. The application of AI are vast and continuously expanding, ranging from health care and finance to transportation system and amusement. In health care, AI is being used to improve diagnostic truth, discover new drug, and personalize intervention plan. In finance, AI-powered algorithm are used for high-frequency trade, imposter sensing, and recognition marking. In transportation system, AI is driving promotion in self-driving car, dealings direction system, and logistics optimization. In the amusement manufacture, AI is being used to create realistic virtual fictional character, bring forth euphony and fine art, and enhance gambling experience. Alongside the numerous benefit of AI, there are also concern and ethical consideration. These include issue related to occupation supplanting, privateers, biased algorithm, and the potential abuse of AI technology. As AI continues to advance, it is important to ensure that its evolution and deployment are guided by ethical principle and regulation to maximize the benefit while minimizing the hazard. In decision, AI has come a long manner since its origin and has emerged as a transformative engineering with diverse application. From narrow AI that specializes in specific undertaking to the chase of general AI that replicates human intelligence service, the battlefield continues to advance rapidly. The key component of AI, including simple machine acquisition, natural linguistic communication process, computing machine sight, and robotics, enable machine to think, ground, realize, and

interact with the universe in slipway that were once unimaginable. While the application of AI hold great hope, it is crucial to
address the ethical consideration associated with its usage to
ensure that it is harnessed responsibly for the welfare of club.

HISTORY AND DEVELOPMENT

The account and evolution of artificial intelligence service, blockchain, and quantum computing have been shaped by a serial of technological promotion and discovery. AI service has its root in the mid-20th hundred, with the coming of computer and the nativity of cognitive scientific discipline. In the 1950s and 1960s, early pioneer such as Alan Turing and toilet Mary McCarthy laid the basis for the battlefield by proposing the thought of a simple machine that could simulate human intelligence service. These early attempt led to the evolution of computing machine plan capable of performing undertaking that required human intelligence service, such as playing cheat or solving complex mathematical problem. The battlefield of artificial intelligence service experienced significant advancement and enlargement in the 1990s and early 2000s, thanks to the coming of big information and promotion in simple machine acquisition algorithm. With the power to procedure and analyze vast sum of information, computer became increasingly capable of learning and making decision without explicit human scheduling. This led to the evolution of artificial neural network and deep acquisition algorithm, which revolutionized the battlefield and gave ascent to the AI application we see nowadays, such as vocalization acknowledgment, mental image categorization, and natural linguistic communication process. Blockchain engineering, on the other minus, has a more recent account, emerging in 2008 with the issue of a white composition by an anonymous individual or grouping of citizenry known as Satoshi Nakamoto. This white composition introduced the conception of a decentralized and immutable Leger, which formed the base of what we now know as blockchain. The first execution of blockchain engineering came with the launching of Bitcoin, a digital correctness that enabled procure and transparent minutes without the demand for a central authorization. Since then, blockchain engineering has evolved rapidly, with the evolution of other cryptocurrencies, such as Ethereum, and the geographic expedition of its potential beyond finance. Blockchain is now being utilized in various industry, including provision concatenation direction, health care, and voting system, to ensure transparency, protection, and immutableness of information. The evolution of smart contract, which are self-executing contract with the footing written into the codification, has further expanded the possibility of blockchain engineering, enabling the mechanization of minutes and reducing the demand for mediator. Quantum computer science, the newest of the three technology, has its root in quantum mechanism, a subdivision of natural philosophy that survey the behavior of atom at the atomic and subatomic degree. In the early 1980s, physicist Richard Feynman proposed the thought of using quantum system to perform calculation more efficiently than classical computer. It was not until the nineties that significant advancement was made in edifice and manipulating quantum spot, or qubits, the fundamental edifice block of quantum computer. Over the past few decades, scientist and engineer have made significant pace in the evolution of quantum computer. While early quantum computer were limited in footing of the figure of qubits and their staleness, recent promotion have led to the creative activity of more powerful and stable quantum system. Company like IBM, google, and Microsoft are actively working on developing practical quantum computer and exploring their potential application, which include solving complex optimization problem, simulating quantum system, and enhancing simple machine learning algorithm. In decision, the account and evolution of artificial intelligence service, blockchain, and quantum computing have been driven by a combining of scientific discovery, technological promotion, and the demand for more efficient and secure computing system. AI service has evolved from its early beginning to become an integral portion of our daily life, powering application ranging from personal assistant to autonomous vehicle. Blockchain engineering, starting with the launching of Bitcoin, has expanded to provide solution in various sectors, enhancing transparency and protection. Quantum computer science, while still in its early phase, shows great hope in revolutionizing computer science and tackling complex problem that are beyond the capability of classical computer. As this technology continue to advance and converge, their potential for transforming industry and club as a unit is vast and exciting.

APPLICATIONS OF AI

The potential application of artificial intelligence are vast and far-reaching, with the potential to revolutionize various aspects of our life. One country in which AI has found significant practical application is in the battlefield of health care. AI-powered algorithm have the paleness to analyze vast sum of affected role information, enabling health care supplier to make more accurate diagnosis and intervention recommendation. AI can also help with dose find, by simulating the personal effects of various compounds and predicting their officiousness, thereby speeding up the evolution procedure. AI can be utilized in the monitor of patient, as well as in the evolution of assistive technology for person with disability. Another country in which AI has made a major wallop is in the transportation system manufacture. Machine learning algorithm can be used to optimize dealings flowing, thereby reducing over-crowding and improving overall traveling multiplication. Autonomous vehicle, which rely heavily on AI, have the potential to revolutionize the manner we travel. This vehicle can navigate complex route system and make split-second decision, all without human intercession. This not only has the potential to reduce accident and save life but also has the potential to significantly increase efficiency and lessening dealings over-crowding. AI has also found application in the financial sphere, where it has greatly enhanced various procedure. For case, AI-powered algorithm can analyze vast sum of financial information to detect form and make prediction. This can be invaluable in making investing decision and managing hazard. AI can also be used to detect fraudulent activity and cyber menace, by monitoring and analyzing vast sum of information in real-time. In add-on, AI can automate repetitive undertaking such as information introduction and written document process, freeing up human resource for more complex and strategic undertaking. In the battlefield of instruction, AI has the potential to greatly enhance the acquisition see. AI-powered system can customize educational message to cater to the individual need and learning manner of student. Adaptive acquisition platform can analyze information on pupil public presentation and provide personalized recommendation for betterment. Virtual world and augmented world technology, which rely on AI, can create immersive acquisition environment, enabling student to gain practical see and a deeper apprehension of complex concept. The potential application of AI also extend to the battlefield of amusement and gambling. AI-powered algorithm can analyze vast sum of information on exploiter preference and behavior, enabling content Godhead to personalize their offer and enhance user experience. Chatbots and virtual assistant, which rely on AI, can also provide amusement and improve exploiter interaction in various application. In the battlefield of agribusiness, AI has the potential to revolutionize farming practice. AI-powered system can analyze information on dirt weather, weather condition form, and harvest output to optimize farming technique and increase productiveness. Machine learning algorithm can also analyze image captured by drone or satellite to detect harvest disease or plague, enabling farmer to take timely activity and minimize output losings. AI-powered automaton can perform un-

48

dertaking such as harvest, snip, and plant, thereby reducing labor cost and increasing efficiency. AI also has the potential to revolutionize the battlefield of client religious service. AI-powered chatbots can provide immediate aid to customer, answering their question and providing solution to common problem. Natural linguistic communication process algorithm enable chatbots to understand and respond to human linguistic communication in a conversational mode. Sentiment analytic thinking algorithm can analyze client feedback and opinion on social medium platform, enabling business to gain valuable penetration and make necessary improvement. In decision, the potential application of AI are broad and diverse, with the potential to revolutionize various industry. From health care and transportation system to finance, instruction, amusement, agribusiness, and client religious service, AI has the potential to greatly enhance procedure and improve overall efficiency. While there are concerns and ethical consideration surrounding the execution of AI, the benefit it brings cannot be ignored. Continual inquiry and evolution in AI will be crucial in harnessing its full potentiality and ensuring the responsible and ethical usage of this powerful engineering.

MACHINE LEARNING

Machine acquisition is a key constituent of artificial intelligence service that has revolutionized various industry and discipline by enabling computer to learn from information without explicit scheduling. With the tremendous growing of digital information in recent old age, simple machine learning algorithm have proven to be instrumental in the analytic thinking and origin of valuable penetration from vast and complex datasets. This powerful instrument has found numerous application in diverse fields including finance, health care, selling, and transportation system. In finance, for case, simple machine learning algorithm have been leveraged to make trade decision, observe imposter, and predict marketplace tendency. Healthcare professional are utilizing simple machine learning algorithm to diagnose disease, develop personalized intervention plan, and predict patient result. Similarly, seller are benefiting from simple machine acquisition by using it to analyze client behavior and preference, thereby enhancing their power to create targeted ad political campaign. Simple machine acquisition algorithm are being employed in transportation system to improve dealings direction, optimize path, and develop autonomous vehicle. The procedure of simple machine acquisition can be broadly categorized into three major type : supervised acquisition, unsupervised acquisition, and support acquisition. In supervised acquisition, the algorithmic rule is provided with labeled information, consisting of input-output pair, from which it learns to predict the end product based on the input signal. This character of acquisition is commonly used for undertaking such as categorization and arrested development. Unsupervised acquisition, on the other minus, deal with unlabeled information, where the algorithmic rule is tasked with finding form and structure within the information without any predefined label. This character of acquisition is particularly useful for undertaking such as bunch and anomaly sensing. Reinforcement learning involves a factor that interacts with an (environs), learning to make decision based on receiving wages or punishment. This character of acquisition is utilized in application where the optimal decision-making scheme is not explicitly known, and the factor must explore its environs to determine the best course of study of activity. One of the key challenge in simple machine acquisition is the number of overfitting, which occurs when a theoretical account is excessively complex and perform well on training information, but fails to generalize to new, unseen information. To mitigate this job, various technique such as regularization and cross-validation are employed. Regularization imposes punishment on theoretical account complexes to prevent overfitting, while cross-validation involves splitting the information into multiple subset for preparation and rating, ensuring that the theoretical account performs well on unseen information. The pick of the right algorithmic rule is crucial in achieving optimal consequence. Different algorithm have different strength and failing, and selecting the appropriate one depends on the specific undertaking at minus, the available information, and computational resource. Another significant dispute in simple machine acquisition is the number of prejudice and equity. Machine acquisition model are trained on historical information, which can often reflect societal bias, leading to biased prediction and decision. For case, in hiring procedure, biased algorithm can inadvertently discriminate against certain group, perpetuating inequality in the work force. Addressing this number requires a careful scrutiny of the preparation information, characteristic technology to remove or mitigate bias, and the evolution of fairness-aware algorithm that explicitly consider fairness constraint during theoretical account preparation and rating. Despite these challenge, simple machine acquisition continues to advance rapidly, driven by progress in computational powerless, handiness of large datasets, and discovery in algorithmic technique. Deep acquisition, a subfield of simple machine acquisition, has gained significant attending in recent old age due to its power to learn hierarchical representation of information using neural network with multiple layer. This has enabled remarkable accomplishment in various spheres, including computing machine sight, natural linguistic communication process, and speech acknowledgment. Deep acquisition technique often requires vast sum of labeled information and substantial computational resource, which may pose challenge in some application. As simple machine learning continues to evolve and permeate various aspects of club, it is essential to address the ethical deduction and societal wallop of this technology. Increasing mechanization facilitated by simple machine acquisition has the potential to displace occupation and exacerbate income inequality. Privacy concern also arises due to the copiousness of personal information being collected and processed. Striking a proportion between invention and upholding ethical principle is necessary to ensure that the benefit of simple machine acquisition are realized while mitigating potential hazard. In decision, simple machine acquisition is a powerful instrument that has transformed numerous industry by enabling computer to learn from information without explicit scheduling. Its application span across finance, health care, selling, transportation system, and many other fields. Machine acquisition can be categorized into supervised acquisition, unsupervised acquisition, and support acquisition, each serving different purpose. Challenge such as overfitting and bias be in simple machine acquisition, requiring technique like regularization and fairness-aware algorithm to mitigate them. As engineering progress, deep acquisition has gained attending, but question about the handiness of labeled information and computational resource originate. Ethical consideration regarding occupation supplanting, income inequality, and privateers also need to be addressed as simple machine learning continues to impact club.

NATURAL LANGUAGE PROCESSING

Natural language processing is a subfield of artificial intelligence service that deal with the fundamental interaction between computer and world through natural linguistic communication. It focuses on developing algorithms and technique that enable computer to understand, interpret, and generate human linguistic communication in a meaningful manner. Natural language processing plays a crucial function in various application such as simple machine interlingual rendition, opinion analytic thinking, vocalization assistant, and info recovery, to name a few. One of the key challenge in natural language processing is the equivocalness of human linguistic communication. Words and phrase can have multiple meaning depending on the linguistic context, making it difficult for computer to accurately understand the intended content. To tackle this dispute, research worker in natural language processing employ various technique such as syntactic and semantic analytic thinking, statistical model, and simple machine acquisition algorithm. These technique help computer to identify and interpret the grammatical construction of sentence, extract meaningful info, and make accurate prediction based on the linguistic context. Statistical model play a vital function in many natural language processing undertaking. These model are trained on large datasets that contain example of human linguistic communication, allowing them to learn form and regularity in linguistic communication use. By analyzing the accompaniment of lyric and phrase, statistical model can predict the likeliness of a specific news given its linguistic context. This enables computer to generate meaningful and coherent sentence that resemble human linguistic communication. Statistical model can be used for undertaking such as part-of-speech tag, where each news in a conviction is assigned a specific grammatical function based on its linguistic context. Machine learning algorithm have revolutionized natural language processing by enabling computer to automatically learn from information and improve their public presentation over clip. Deep acquisition, a subset of simple machine acquisition, has particularly shown remarkable consequence in natural language processing undertaking. Deep acquisition model, such as recurrent neural network (RNNs) and transformer model, can process sequence of lyric and gaining control composite form in linguistic communication. These model have achieved state-of-the-art public presentation in undertaking such as simple machine interlingual rendition, linguistic communication coevals, and opinion analytic thinking. Another important facet of natural language processing is the power to understand and generate human-like response in conversation. This battlefield, known as dialog system or chatbots, purpose to create computing machine plan that can engage in natural conversation with world. Building effective dialog system requires a deep apprehension of natural linguistic communication and the power to generate consistent and contextually appropriate response. To achieve this, research worker in natural language processing usage technique such as sequence-to-sequence mold, support acquisition, and linguistic communication mold. Natural language processing is also instrumental in info recovery undertaking, where computer procedure and extract relevant info from large volume of unstructured information. This is particularly useful in sphere such as web hunt, where the end is to provide exact and relevant info to user based on their question. Natural language processing technique can be used to analyze the significance and purpose behind user question, identify relevant document and entanglement page, and rank them based on their relevancy to the question. Natural linguistic communication apprehension and info origin technique are also crucial in undertaking such as text summarization, where the end is to generate concise summary of long text. Despite the promotion in natural language processing, challenge still remain. One of the key challenge is the deficiency of labeled information for preparation model. Many natural language processing undertaking require large sum of labeled information, which can be expensive and time-consuming to obtain. Natural language processing model often struggles with apprehension nuanced linguistic communication use, slang expression, and cultural mention, which vary across different region and community. Understanding and effectively processing this aspect of linguistic communication present ongoing challenge for natural language processing research worker. In decision, natural linguistic communication process plays a vital function in enabling computer to understand, interpret, and generate human linguistic communication in a meaningful manner. Through the usage of various technique such as statistical model and simple machine acquisition algorithm, natural language processing has made significant promotion in undertaking such as simple machine interlingual rendition, opinion analytic thinking, vocalization assistant, and info recovery. Challenge such as the equivocalness of human linguistic communication and the deficiency of labeled information still remain, pushing research worker to continually introduce and improve the capability of natural language processing. With further pro-motion, natural linguistic communication process has the potential to revolutionize how computer interact with world and the manner we communicate with engineering.

ROBOTICS

Robotics, which is the subdivision of engineering focused on creating intelligent machine that are capable of performing undertaking autonomously or with minimal human intercession, has emerged as a pivotal battlefield with immense potentiality in various industry. The promotion in robotics have paved the manner for the integrating of artificial intelligence service and simple machine acquisition algorithm, enabling automaton to learn and adapt to their milieu. Through the usage of detector, actuator, and control condition system, automaton can interact with their environs, execute complex undertaking, and make autonomous decision. This paleness has revolutionized industry such as fabrication, health care, agribusiness, and even infinite geographic expedition. In the fabrication manufacture, robotics has played a crucial function in increasing productiveness and efficiency. Automatize robotic system can perform repetitive, physically demanding, and dangerous undertaking with preciseness and velocity, minimizing mistake and reducing the hazard of accident. This has led to improved merchandise caliber, reduced product cost, and increased profitableness for manufacturer. Robotic weaponry equipped with advanced sight system and artificial intelligence service algorithm can perceive and manipulate object with high truth, enabling them to handle intricate fabrication undertaking that were once reserved for human worker. As a consequence, world can focus on more complex and creative aspect of product, enhancing overall productiveness. The health care manufacture has also embraced robotics to improve affected role attention and result. Surgical automaton, for case, have revolutionized minimally invasive procedure by providing surgeon with enhanced manual dexterity, preciseness, and visual image capability. This robotic system can perform complex surgery through small incision, resulting in reduced injury, shorter infirmary corset, and faster convalescence multiplication for patient. Automaton have been deployed in reclamation setting to assist patient with physical therapy, helping them regain mobility and independence. By leveraging robotics, healthcare supplier can enhance the caliber and handiness of treatment, especially in remote control or underserved are agribusiness is another sphere that has witnessed the transformative wallop of robotics. The usage of autonomous automaton in agriculture has the potential to revolutionize traditional agricultural practice. For case, automaton can be deployed in preciseness agribusiness technique, where they can autonomously monitor crop, collect information on dirt weather, and optimize irrigation and fertilization procedure. This not only improves the efficiency of farming trading operations but also reduces resourcefulness wastage, minimizes environmental wallop, and enhances harvest output. The usage of automaton in harvest and sorting undertaking can alleviate labor deficit and ensure timely and accurate green goods aggregation, thereby improving the overall provision concatenation efficiency. The geographic expedition of outer infinite is another frontier where robotics has excelled. Robotic wanderer and probe have been sent to various celestial body, such as Red Planet, to gather scientific information and image. This automaton can navigate challenging terrain, analyze geological sample, and convey valuable info back to earth. The power to remotely explore and study distant planet and asteroid through robotics has provided scientist with invaluable penetration into the beginning of the existence and the passiveness of extraterrestrial living. Human-robot coaction in infinite mission is becoming increasingly important, as robotic system can assist astronaut in performing complex undertaking, conducting experiment, and mitigating hazard during spacewalk. While the potential benefit of robotics are undeniably vast, there are also concern that originate with its integrating into club. The widespread acceptance of robotics could lead to break in the labor marketplace, as mechanization replace certain occupation, creating unemployment and inequality. Ethical consideration surrounding the usage of automaton in sensitive industry like health care and military demand to be thoroughly addressed to ensure the refuge, privateers, and wellbeing of person. In decision, the battlefield of robotics has emerged as a powerful enabler, bringing together artificial intelligence service, simple machine acquisition, and advanced sensing capability to create intelligent machine capable of performing a diverse scope of undertaking. From improving productiveness in fabrication and enhancing affected role attention in health care to transforming agribusiness practice and exploring outer infinite, the application of robotics are vast and far-reaching. While there are concerns regarding the societal deduction of widespread mechanization, robotics undoubtedly holds immense potentiality for revolutionizing various industry and enhancing the caliber of human living. As engineering continues to advance, it is crucial for research worker, policymakers, and stakeholder to collaborate in order of magnitude to harness the transformative powerless of robotics responsibly and ethically.

IMPACT OF AI ON SOCIETY

The wallop of AI on club is profound and far-reaching. As AI technology continue to advance, they have the potential to revolutionize various aspects of our daily life, from health care to transportation system to amusement. One of the most significant impact of AI is in the battlefield of health care. With the power to procedure and analyze vast sum of medical information, AI has the potentiality to improve diagnosing and intervention, leading to more accurate and personalized health care. For illustration, AI algorithm can analyze medical image, such as X-ray and magnetic resonance imaging, and detect abnormality that might be missed by human doctor. This can lead to earlier sensing of disease and potentially life-saving intervention. AI can also be used to develop personalized intervention plan based on a person's unique genetic make-up and medical account, maximizing the effectivity of treatment while minimizing side personal effects. In add-on to healthcare, AI is also transforming the transportation system manufacture. Autonomous vehicle, powered by AI technology, have the potential to make our roadway safer and more efficient. AI algorithm can analyze real-time information from detector and camera, enabling self-driving car to navigate complex dealings situation and make split-second decision. This can dramatically reduce the figure of accident caused by human mistake and improve dealings flowing, ultimately saving life and reducing over-crowding. AI is revolutionizing the amusement manufacture. AI algorithm can analyze vast sum of information about consumer preference and behavior, allowing company to personalize their offer and deliver more relevant and engaging message. This is evident in streaming platform like Netflix, which uses AI to recommend movie and television show based on individual screening habit and preference. AI can also be used to create more immersive and realistic virtual world experience, enhancing the amusement economic value of video game and interactive medium. While the wallop of AI on club is undoubtedly transformative, it is not without its challenge and hazard. One of the main concern surrounding AI is its potential wallop on employ. As AI technologies become more advanced, there is a fearfulness that they will replace human worker in various industry, leading to widespread occupation deprivation and economic imbalance. This is particularly true for occupation that involve routine and repetitive undertaking, which can be easily automated by AI algorithm. It is important to note that AI also has the potential to create new occupation and opportunity. As AI technology continue to evolve, there will be a growing requirement for professional with expertness in AI-related fields, such as simple machine acquisition and information analytic thinking. AI can augment human capability, allowing person to focus on more complex and creative undertaking that require human judgement and hunch. The wallop of AI on employ is likely to be complex and nuanced, requiring a careful proportion between mechanization and human engagement. Another care surrounding AI is its potential wallop on privateers and protection. AI algorithms rely on vast sum of information to learn and make prediction, raising question about the possession and control condition of personal info. As AI technologies become more prevalent, it will be crucial to establish robust regulation and precaution to protect person privateers and ensure the responsible usage of AI. AI is not immune to bias and favoritism. AI algorithm are trained on historical information, which can reflect existing societal bias and inequality. If not carefully designed and monitored, AI system can perpetuate and amplify these bias, leading to unfair result and exacerbating social inequality. Addressing these bias and ensuring the ethical usage of AI will be critical for minimizing the negative social impact of AI technology. In decision, the wallop of AI on club is extensive and transformative. From health care to transportation system to amusement, AI technology have the potential to revolutionize various aspects of our daily life, improving efficiency, truth, and personalization. This wallop is not without its challenge and hazard. Concern about employ, privateers, protection, and bias must be carefully addressed to maximize the benefit of AI while minimizing its negative social impact. With proper regulation and ethical consideration, AI has the potential to create a more inclusive and equitable club.

JOB AUTOMATION

Occupation mechanization is a subject that has gained significant attending in recent old age, as promotion in AI, blockchain engineering, and quantum computing have rapidly transformed various industry. The conception of occupation mechanization mention to the usage of engineering, particularly AI, to perform undertaking that were previously done by world. While occupation mechanization has the potential to increase productiveness and efficiency, it also raises concern about the supplanting of human worker and the deduction for the hereafter of piece of work. One of the primary driver of occupation mechanization is AI, which has made significant pace in recent old age. AI is the computer simulation of human intelligence service in machine that are programmed to think and learn, enabling them to perform undertaking that traditionally required human intelligence service. AI technology, such as simple machine acquisition and natural linguistic communication process, have made significant advancement in area such as client religious service, information analytic thinking, and even creative undertaking like writing and designing. As AI system become more sophisticated and capable, they have the potential to replace human worker in a wide scope of industry. Blockchain engineering is another emerging engineering that is expected to have a significant wallop on occupation mechanization. Blockchain is a decentralized digital Leger that record minutes across multiple computer, making it a crystalline and secure manner to store and verify information. The usage of blockchain engineering can streamline procedure in various industry, such as provision concatenation direction, finance, and health care. By eliminating the demand for mediator and enabling procure and transparent minutes, blockchain has the potential to automate many undertaking that were previously done by world, such as declaration direction and personal identity confirmation. Quantum computer science is yet another technological promotion that has the potential to revolutionize occupation mechanization. Quantum computing leverages the principle of quantum mechanism to perform complex calculation at an unprecedented velocity. This engineering has the potential to solve problem that are currently intractable for classical computer and has application in various fields, including cryptanalysis, optimization, and dose find. As quantum computing continues to advance, it has the potential to automate complex calculation and information analytic thinking undertaking that were previously done by world, leading to increased productiveness and efficiency. While occupation mechanization has the potential to bring numerous benefit, there are also concern about its wallop on the labor marketplace. One of the primary concern is the supplanting of human worker, as machine and AI system take over undertaking that were traditionally done by world. This supplanting can lead to occupation losings and unemployment, particularly for worker in industry that are susceptible to mechanization, such as fabrication and client religious service. The ascent of occupation mechanization could increase income inequality, as worker with lower accomplishment degree may struggle to find employ in a highly automated economic system. Occupation mechanization raises question about the hereafter of piece of work and the skill required in the digital historic period. As machine and AI system become more capable, the skill that are in requirement in the labor market-place are likely to change. In order of magnitude to thrive in an automated economic system, worker will need to develop skill that are difficult to automate, such as problem-solving, critical thought, and creativeness. There is a growing demand for worker to have a strong base in root (scientific discipline, engineering, technology, and math) fields, as this skill are becoming increasingly important in the digital historic period. To mitigate the potential negative impact of occupation mechanization, there is a demand for proactive policy and investing in instruction and retrain. Government and policymakers should work to ensure that worker have entrée to the necessary instruction and preparation plan to acquire the skill needed in an automated economic system. Attempt should be made to foster invention and entrepreneurship, as new technology and industry emerge in the aftermath of occupation mechanization. By taking a proactive attack, club can harness the potentiality of occupation mechanization while minimizing its negative impact. In decision, occupation mechanization is a transformative tendency that is being driven by promotion in AI, blockchain engineering, and quantum computer science. While occupation mechanization has the potential to increase productiveness and efficiency, it also raises concern about the supplanting of human worker and the hereafter of piece of work. To address these concern, proactive policy and investing in instruction and retraining are necessary to ensure that worker are prepared for the challenge and opportunity of an automated economic system. By doing so, club can harness the transformative powerless of occupation mechanization while minimizing its negative impact.

ETHICAL CONSIDERATIONS

Ethical consideration play a crucial function in the evolution and execution of AI, blockchain, and quantum computer science. As this technology continue to evolve and become more integrated into our club, it is essential to consider the ethical deduction that they bring. One primary ethical care originate from the potential abuse of AI algorithm. AI system have the power to mine vast sum of information and make autonomous decision, which can have far-reaching consequence. For illustration, biased algorithm can perpetuate favoritism and inequality, as they replicate and amplify the bias present in the information they are trained on. In order of magnitude to mitigate this hazard, it is imperative for developer and policymakers to implement strict guideline and regulation to ensure that AI system are fair, transparent, and accountable. The number of privateers and information protective covering arises with the integrating of blockchain engineering. While blockchain offer a decentralized and transparent political platform for minutes and information storehouse, it also challenges traditional impression of privateers. The immutableness and permanency of blockchain record raise concern about the storehouse and use of personal and sensitive info. Ethical consideration should guide the designing and execution of blockchain system to safeguard the privateers of person while harnessing its benefit. The evolution of quantum computing raise ethical concern regarding cybersecurity and national protection. Quantum computer have the potential to break current encoding algorithm, which could undermine the protection of sensitive info and critical substructure. As quantum computer science advancement, ethical consideration demand that attempt be made to bolster cybersecurity measure and develop quantum-resistant encoding algorithm to ensure the protective covering of information. The ethical deduction of the unequal entrée to this technology cannot be ignored. The digital watershed, already a significant number, could be further exacerbated by promotion in AI, blockchain, and quantum computer science. Without adequate measure to address this disparity, marginalized community and developing state could be left behind, widening social and economic inequality. Ethical consideration should drive attempt to bridge this watershed and ensure equitable entrée to this technology. The wallop of AI and mechanization on employ and work force kinetics raises important ethical consideration. As AI engineering continues to advance, there is a legitimate care about occupation supplanting and the potential deprivation of support. While AI has the potential to increase efficiency and productiveness, it also threatens certain occupation sector, particularly those that require repetitive and routine undertaking. It is crucial for club to anticipate and address the ethical deduction of mechanization, such as retraining plan and social refuge internet, to support the work force in transitioning to new and meaningful employ. The ethical consideration of the ethical and responsible usage of information cannot be overlooked. With the increasing trust on information for decision-making, there is a demand to ensure that information aggregation, storehouse, and use adhere to strict ethical standard. This includes obtaining informed except from person, protecting personal and sensitive info, and preventing the abuse or maltreatment of information.

Organization and policymakers must establish robust information administration model and regulation to uphold the ethical usage of information in the epoch of AI, blockchain, and quantum computer science. In decision, ethical consideration are overriding in the evolution and execution of AI, blockchain, and quantum computer science. Addressing these concern is essential to ensure that this technology are used responsibly and for the improvement of club. By taking a proactive attack to ethical motive, policymakers, developer, and research worker can harness the transformative potentiality of this technology while mitigating their possible hazard and negative impact. Only by consistently evaluating and reevaluating the ethical deduction, can we ensure a hereafter where AI, blockchain, and quantum computing lend positively to our life.

AI IN HEALTHCARE AND MEDICINE

AI has the potential to revolutionize and transform the health care and medical specialty sphere in unprecedented slipway. The integrating of AI technology in healthcare system can enhance the truth and efficiency of topology, enable personalized treatment, improve affected role result, and ultimately, save life. One of the key application of AI in health care is in medical imagination, where deep acquisition algorithm can analyze large volume of medical image and detect abnormality with higher truth than human radiologist. For case, in a survey conducted by google health and the northwestern university in 2020, an AI scheme demonstrated superior public presentation in chest malignant neoplastic disease sensing compared to human expert. Another country where AI can make a significant wallop is in dose find and evolution. The traditional dose find procedure is lengthy, expensive, and often involves high loser rate. AI-powered algorithm can analyze vast sum of information, such as genomic and proteomics information, to identify potential dose target and optimize the designing of new compound. This can streamline the dose find procedure, accelerate the evolution of novel therapy, and potentially lead to more effective treatment for disease. In add-on, AI can also contribute to improving affected role attention through predictive analytics. By analyzing affected role information, AI algorithm can identify form and tendency that may predict disease patterned advance or adverse event, allowing healthcare supplier to intervene early and provide appropriate intervention. AI-powered chatbots and virtual assistant can provide round-the-clock reinforcement by answering common medical question, offering basic medical advice, and reminding patient to take their medicine. These AI-driven application hold immense potentiality for enhancing healthcare handiness and improving patient result, especially in region with limited health care substructure. The widespread acceptance of AI in health care also raises ethical and legal concern that must be addressed. For case, the usage of AI in making medical decision raises question about answerability and duty. Who should be held liable if an AI algorithmic rule makes a wrong diagnosing or recommends a wrong intervention ? The deficiency of transparency and interpretability of some AI model also raises concern about their dependability and potential bias. The aggregation and usage of affected role information by AI system raise privateers and protection concern, particularly with the increasing edification of cyber menace. Addressing these challenge requires the evolution of robust regulatory model and ethical guideline that proportion invention and patient refuge. In decision, the convergence of AI, blockchain, and quantum computing holds immense potentiality for transforming various sectors, including finance, provision concatenation direction, and health care. AI technology can enhance decision-making, improve operational efficiency, and facilitate the creative activity of new digital ecosystem. Blockchain can enable procure and transparent minutes, streamline procedure, and enhance reliance and answerability. Quantum computing can revolutionize computing powerless and velocity, enabling complex calculation and simulation that were previously impossible. The widespread acceptance of this technology also presents various challenge, including regulatory, ethical, and protection concern. To realize the full potentiality of AI, blockchain, and quantum computer science, coaction among various stakeholders, including government, manufacture, academe, and civil club, is essential. This coaction should focus on addressing the associated challenge, developing ethical model, and ensuring that this technology are deployed in a mode that is inclusive, sustainable, and respect human right. By harnessing the transformative powerless of AI, blockchain, and quantum computer science, club can unlock new possibility, create innovative solution to complex problem, and pave the manner towards a more digital and connected hereafter. Another invention that is shaping the hereafter is quantum computing. Unlike traditional computer, which utilize spot for information storehouse and process, quantum computer work with quantum spot, or qubits. These qubits can exist in multiple state simultaneously, thanks to a rule of quantum mechanism called principle of superposition. This allows quantum computer to perform complex calculation at a much faster charge per unit than their classical counterpart. Quantum computer have the power to solve problem that are currently unsolvable with classical computer due to their immense computational powerless. Quantum computer science has the potential to revolutionize various industry. For case, in the battlefield of medical specialty, quantum computer can be employed to solve complex genetic and protein folding problem, which could lead to the evolution of more effective drug and treatment for disease. In the financial sphere, quantum computer science could facilitate the analytic thinking of vast sum of information, enabling more accurate prediction and hazard appraisal. Quantum computer could greatly enhance the capability of artificial intelligence service system, as they would be able to process and analyze huge sum of information in real-time. Quantum computer science is still in its babyhood, and there are numerous challenge that need to be overcome before its true potentiality can be realized. One of the main hurdling is the number of qubit staleness. Quantum system are extremely fragile and can be easily affected by external perturbation, such as temperature or electromagnetic radiation sickness. Maintaining the staleness of qubits is crucial for the achiever of quantum computer science. Another dispute is scaling up the figure of qubits. Currently, quantum computer are limited to a few twelve qubits, which severely restricts their computational powerless. Overcoming this scalability number is essential for the evolution of larger and more powerful quantum computer. In order of magnitude to tackle these challenge, scientist and research worker are exploring different approach to quantum computer science. One promise boulevard is the usage of topological qubits, which are more robust against external dissonance and perturbation. Topological qubits are based on the principle of regional anatomy, a subdivision of math that survey the property of infinite that are preserved under continuous transformation. These qubits are less susceptible to mistake caused by environmental factor, making them more reliable for quantum computer science application. Another attack to quantum computer science is the evolution of quantum annealing system, which are specifically designed to solve optimization problem. Quantum tempering is a proficiency that leverages quantum fluctuation to find the lowest free energy province of a mathematical function, which corresponds to the optimal answer of a job. Quantum annealing system have been successfully applied to various optimization problems, such as portfolio optimization and dose find. Research worker are investigating the usage of trapped ion qubits, which are highly stable and can be controlled with great preciseness. Trapped ion qubits are based on the use of individual ion trapped in an electromagnetic battlefield. These qubits have shown promising consequence in footing of their staleness and scalability, making them a potential campaigner for future quantum computing system. In decision, artificial intelligence service, blockchain, and quantum computer science are three invention that are driving the hereafter of engineering. AI service is transforming industry and revolutionizing the manner we live and piece of work. Blockchain engineering is revolutionizing the manner we handle minutes and ensuring transparency and protection. Quantum computer science has the potential to solve currently unsolvable problem and revolutionize various fields, such as medical specialty and finance. While this invention present numerous challenge, scientist and research worker are actively working towards overcoming them and harnessing the full potentiality of this technology. The hereafter is exciting, and this technology will undoubtedly play a crucial function in shaping it.

III. BLOCKCHAIN TECHNOLOGY

Blockchain technology Blockchain engineering is one of the most fascinating and disruptive technological promotion of the 21st hundred. With its decentralized and transparent nature, it has the potential to revolutionize infinite industry, from finance and provision concatenation direction to healthcare and authorities. At its nucleus, blockchain is a distributed Leger that enables to procure and immutable storehouse of information. The engineering gained its popularity through the outgrowth of cryptocurrencies, such as Bitcoin. Blockchain is more than just a digital correctness ; it is a powerful instrument that can solve various challenge faced by traditional centralized system. One of the key feature of blockchain engineering is decentralization. Unlike traditional centralized system, where information is stored and controlled by a single entity, blockchain enables the statistical distribution of information across a web of computer (node) . Each knob on the web maintains a transcript of the entire blockchain, making it extremely difficult for any individual or organization to tamper with the information. This decentralization ensures the unity and protection of the info stored on the blockchain. Consensus mechanism, such as proof-of-work or proof-of-stake, are employed to validate and verify minutes within the web, further enhancing the protection and rustiness of the scheme. Another significant feature of blockchain is its transparency. All minutes recorded on the blockchain are visible to every player on the web. This transparency promotes reliance and answerability, as any player can audit and verify the minutes. The immutableness of the blockchain ensures that once a dealing is recorded, it cannot be altered or erased. This characteristic makes blockchain especially valuable in industry where information unity is crucial, such as provision concatenation direction and health care. By providing a crystalline and immutable phonograph record of minutes, blockchain engineering can enhance reliance and traceability throughout various procedure. The potential application of blockchain engineering are vast and diverse. In the financial manufacture, blockchain can revolutionize remittance, cross-border payment, and even the issue of digital currency by central Banks. By eliminating mediator and increasing efficiency, blockchain can significantly reduce dealing cost and improve financial inclusivity. The decentralized nature of blockchain can mitigate the hazard of imposter and enhance the protection of financial minutes. Supply concatenation direction is another sphere that can benefit greatly from blockchain engineering. The distributed Leger scheme can provide real-time nimbleness into the entire provision concatenation procedure, from the beginning of raw material to the final merchandise. This transparency allows for swift designation and declaration of any issue, such as forgery merchandise or delay in bringing. The immutableness of the blockchain ensures the genuineness and unity of the merchandise throughout the provision concatenation. These feature can help build reliance among consumer and improve the overall efficiency of the provision concatenation. The health care manufacture is ripe for break by blockchain engineering. Medical record, being highly sensitive and confidential, are often scattered across multiple health care supplier and are prone to breach and mistake. By leveraging blockchain, patient can have complete control condition over their medical information, granting license to supplier to entrée their record. Blockchain's decentralized and secure nature can enhance the privateers and protection of medical info, while also improving the interoperability and efficiency of healthcare system. Blockchain can facilitate clinical test and inquiry by securely storing and sharing information among research worker and organization. Government around the universe are also exploring the potentiality of blockchain engineering. By utilizing blockchain for voting system, authorities agency can ensure transparent and tamper-proof election. Land register can leverage blockchain to ensure the unity and transparency of belongings possession record. Blockchain can also be utilized in personal identity direction, providing person with more control condition over their personal information and reducing the hazard of personal identity larceny. This application demonstrate the potentiality of blockchain to enhance administration, improve reliance, and streamline administrative procedure. In decision, blockchain engineering has the potential to reshape various industry by decentralizing and providing transparency in minutes. This invention has the powerless to revolutionize finance, provision concatenation direction, health care, and administration, among many other sectors. By eliminating mediator and enhancing protection, blockchain can improve efficiency, reduce cost, and build reliance among participant. As the engineering continues to mature and evolve, it is crucial for stakeholder across industry to explore and embrace the benefit of blockchain, laying the basis for a more decentralized, transparent, and efficient hereafter.

EXPLANATION OF BLOCKCHAIN

This engineering, often associated with cryptocurrencies like Bitcoin, has gained significant attending in recent old age for its potential to revolutionize various industry. At its nucleus, blockchain is a distributed Leger scheme that allows multiple party to maintain a shared and transparent phonograph record of minutes or information. It is a decentralized web where info is stored in block, which are linked together using cryptographic algorithm to form a concatenation. Each city block contains a cryptographic hashish of the previous city block, effectively creating a chronological order of magnitude of minutes that is virtually impossible to alter retroactively. One of the key feature of blockchain is its power to provide reliance and protection without the demand for a central authorization. Traditional system typically relies on mediator, such as Banks or authorities institution, to verify and validate minutes. In direct contrast, blockchain allows participant to trust the scheme itself rather than relying on an external entity. This is achieved through a consensus chemical mechanism, where participant on the web reach an understanding on the cogency of each dealing before it is added to the blockchain. Various consensus algorithms, such as proof-of-work or proof-of-stake, ensure that minutes are validated in a procured and tamper-resistant mode. Another important facet of blockchain is its immutableness. Once a city block is added to the concatenation, it becomes extremely difficult to alter or delete the information it contains. This is because changing the info within a city block would require modifying all subsequent block as well, which would require a bulk of participant to collude and rewrite the entire blockchain account. This makes blockchain a highly procure and reliable scheme for storing sensitive info, as any effort to tamper with the information would be immediately detectable. Blockchain provides transparency and traceability by making the entire dealing account visible to all participant. Every dealing is recorded on the blockchain and can be accessed and verified by anyone with the necessary permission. This transparency can bring significant benefit in various industry, such as provision concatenation direction, where the beginning and genuineness of merchandise can be easily tracked and verified. It can also enhance the audit procedure, as all minutes are permanently recorded and can be audited in a crystalline and efficient mode. In add-on to its potential application in finance and provision concatenation, blockchain engineering is also being explored in other area such as health care, free energy, and authorities. In the health care manufacture, for illustration, blockchain can enable procure and interoperable wellness record, allowing patient to have control condition over their own information and portion it seamlessly with healthcare supplier. In the free energy sphere, blockchain can facilitate peer-to-peer free energy trade and enable the integrating of renewable free energy beginning into the existing power system. In the authorities sphere, blockchain can enhance the transparency and efficiency of public service, such as vote or belongings enrollment. Despite its numerous potential benefit, blockchain is not without challenge. The engineering is still relatively new and faces scalability issue, as the current blockchain network struggle to handle large sum of minutes. The free energy ingestion of blockchain network, particularly those using proof-of-work consensus algorithm, has raised concern regarding its environmental wallop. The regulatory model surrounding blockchain is still evolving, and state around the universe are grappling with how to effectively govern this emerging engineering. In decision, blockchain engineering holds immense potentiality to revolutionize various industry by providing a decentralized, procure, and crystalline scheme for recording and verifying minutes or information. Its power to establish reliance and protection without the demand for mediator, its immutableness, and its transparency make it a powerful instrument for improving efficiency, reducing imposter, and enhancing answerability. Challenge related to scalability, free energy ingestion, and ordinance must be addressed for blockchain to fully realize its potential and become an integral portion of our digital substructure.

CHARACTERISTICS OF BLOCKCHAIN

Feature of blockchain, the distributed Leger engineering that underlies cryptocurrencies such as Bitcoin, is characterized by several key features that make it unique and promising for various application beyond finance. Firstly, blockchain is decentralized, meaning that there is no central authorization or intermediary controlling the web. Instead, a web of computer, known as node, collectively keep and validate the blockchain, ensuring reliance and protection. This decentralization eliminates the demand for mediator, reduce cost, and increases transparency. Secondly, blockchain is immutable, or tamper-proof. Once a dealing or information is recorded on the blockchain, it cannot be altered or deleted. This is achieved through the usage of cryptographic technique and consensus algorithm, such as proof-of-work or proof-of-stake, which ensure the cogency and unity of the information. The immutableness facet of blockchain is particularly valuable in application that require auditable and verifiable record, such as provision concatenation direction or health care. Blockchain provides transparency and nakedness, as all participant on the web have entrée to the same info. Minutes and information recorded on the blockchain are visible to all participant, reducing the dissymmetry of info that often exists in centralized system. The usage of public and private key for hallmark and encoding adds an extra bed of protection and privateers to blockchain minutes. Another key feature of blockchain is its high grade of protection. Due to the decentralized nature of blockchain, it is extremely difficult for a single entity to compromise the entire web. Each dealing is cryptographically linked to the previous one, forming a concatenation of block that is virtually incorruptible. This characteristic makes blockchain highly resistant to hacking and imposter, making it an attractive answer for application that involve sensitive info, such as personal identity direction or intellectual belongings protective covering. Blockchain provides reliance and answerability without requiring reliance between participant. Traditional system rely on reliance in a central authorization or intermediary to ensure the cogency of minutes and information. In direct contrast, blockchain achieve trust through consensus mechanism, where the bulk of participant in the web hold on the cogency of minutes. This distributed reliance chemical mechanism eliminates the demand for reliance in a single entity and reduces the hazard of imposter or use. Blockchain enable smart contract, which are self-executing contract with predefined rule and weather. Smart contract are coded onto the blockchain and automatically executed when the specified weather is met. This eliminates the demand for mediator in contractual agreement, reducing cost and increasing efficiency. Smart contract have the potential to revolutionize various industry, such as real land, policy, or logistics, by automating complex procedure and reducing the hazard of imposter or dispute. Blockchain is highly scalable and can handle a large figure of minutes. With the coming of technology such as sharing or side chains, blockchain network can scale horizontally, allowing for increased throughput and faster dealing process. This scalability is essential for widespread acceptance of blockchain in application that require high dealing volume, such as defrayal system or provision irons. Blockchain promote interoperability, as it can be integrated with existing system and technology.

Blockchain network can communicate and interoperate with each other using standardized protocol and interface, enabling unlined information interchange and coaction between different organization or platform. This interoperability facet of block-chain is crucial for building a full-bodied and interconnected ecosystem that can leverage the benefit of blockchain across various spheres. In decision, blockchain posse a unique exercise set of feature that make it a promising engineering for a wide scope of application beyond finance. Its decentralization, immutableness, transparency, protection, reliance, scalability, smart contract, and interoperability provide a solid base for developing innovative solution in area such as provision concatenation direction, health care, personal identity direction, or intellectual belongings protective covering. As blockchain continues to evolve and mature, it has the potential to reshape industry and revolutionize how we store, verify, and interchange information and economic value in the digital historic period.

DECENTRALIZATION

Decentralization is a key conception in the fields of AI, blockchain engineering, and quantum computer science. In each of this sphere, the impression of decentralization plays a critical function in enabling invention and establishing reliance. In AI, decentralization mention to the statistical distribution of computing powerless and decision-making across multiple node or device, thereby fostering feebleness, efficiency, and resiliency. This attack minimizes the hazard of a single detail of loser and enhances the overall public presentation of AI system. Blockchain engineering, on the other minus, relies heavily on the conception of decentralization to create reliance and protection in a peer-to-peer web. By distributing the Leger across multiple node, blockchain guarantee transparency, immutableness, and opposition to censorship or unauthorized entrée. Consequently, this engineering has gained significant popularity in various industry, including finance, provision concatenation, and health care. Decentralization holds immense potentiality in quantum computer science, a battlefield that leverages the property of quantum mechanism to solve complex computational problem. The decentralized nature of quantum computer science allows for the statistical distribution of computing resource and therefore enables the collaborative attempt of research worker and institution worldwide. This attack accelerates invention and creates a global community of interests of expert who can collectively unlock the potentiality of quantum computer science. De-

93

centralization serve as a steer rule across this three sphere, revolutionizing the manner we develop and apply advanced technology. In the kingdom of AI, decentralization empower network and algorithm to learn and adapt independently, eliminating the demand for a centralized control condition scheme. By distributing the computational loading among various nodes, AI system can process vast sum of information concurrently, resulting in significantly faster and more efficient decision-making. Decentralization mitigates the hazard of scheme failure or closure caused by a single knob, enhancing the resiliency and hardiness of AI application. For case, in self-driving car, decentralized AI allows vehicle-to-vehicle communicating, enabling real-time decision-making based on local observation and info. This attack not only enhances the refuge and dependability of autonomous vehicle but also fosters a dynamic and adaptive ecosystem of AI-powered transportation system. In the kingdom of blockchain engineering, decentralization plays a crucial function in establishing reliance and protection in a web of peer. By distributing the Leger across multiple node, blockchain guarantee that no single entity has control over the entire scheme. This crystalline and immutable nature of blockchain makes it highly resistant to tampering, imposter, or use. Decentralization enable consensus mechanism like proof-of-work or proof-of-stake, where multiple node participate in verify and validating minutes. This procedure ensures the unity and immutableness of the blockchain, making it a trustworthy political platform for various application. For case, in the financial sphere, decentralized cryptocurrencies like Bitcoin have gained popularity due to their power to facilitate procure and transparent minutes without the demand for mediator like Banks. Similarly, decentralized provision concatenation solution based on blockchain engineering offering enhanced transparency and traceability, enabling consumer to make informed decision based on reliable merchandise info. In the kingdom of quantum computer science, decentralization facilitate collaboration among research worker and institution, enabling the collective geographic expedition and evolution of this cutting-edge engineering. Given the immense complexes and computational powerless required for quantum computer science, decentralization let for the statistical distribution of computing resource, expertness, and cognition across the Earth. This attack encourages coaction, accelerates inquiry advancement, and promote knowledge sharing within the scientific community of interests. Decentralization enables the widening of position and the interchange of diverse idea, which can lead to discovery and promotion in quantum computer science. By fostering a decentralized ecosystem, we can harness the collective powerless of expert and resource to address complex problem and unlock the full potentiality of quantum computing technology. In decision, decentralization is a fundamental conception in the sphere of AI, blockchain engineering, and quantum computer science. It empowers AI system, blockchain network, and quantum computing community to achieve unprecedented degree of efficiency, protection, and coaction. By embracing decentralization, we can revolutionize the manner we build and apply advanced technology, paving the manner for future invention and societal transformation. As this technology continue to evolve, the grandness of decentralization will only increase, shaping the landscape painting of AI, blockchain, and quantum computer science for old age to come.

TRANSPARENCY

Transparency is a crucial facet when it comes to the execution of emerging technology such as artificial intelligence service, blockchain, and quantum computer science. In the kingdom of artificial intelligence service, transparency mention to the power to explain the decision-making procedure of AI system. This is particularly important considering the increasing usage of AI in various application, ranging from health care and finance to criminal justness. With AI making decision that impact person and club as a unit, it becomes imperative to understand how this decision are reached. One of the main challenge in achieving transparency in AI lies in the complexes of AI algorithm. Most AI system, especially those based on deep acquisition technique, are known as black box, meaning they produce consequence of providing any account or justification for this consequence. This deficiency of transparency raises concern about the equity, answerability, and dependability of AI system. For case, AI algorithm may inadvertently encode bias present in the information used for preparation, leading to discriminatory result. In such case, it becomes difficult to understand why a particular determination was made and whether it was influenced by hidden bias. To address these issue, attempt are being made to develop technique that enhance the transparency of AI system. Explainable AI (CAI) is an emerging battlefield that aims to provide explanation for the decision made by AI algorithm. By offering penetration into the decision-making procedure, CAI can help identify bias and ensure that AI system are accountable for their action. Various approach are being explored in CAI, including rule-based model, visual image, and natural linguistic communication coevals. Blockchain engineering, on the other minus, offers inherent transparency through its decentralized and immutable nature. A blockchain is essentially a distributed Leger that record minutes across multiple node, creating a crystalline and tamper-resistant phonograph record of each dealing. This transparency is particularly valuable in application such as provision concatenation direction, financial service, and health care, where reliance and answerability are crucial. By providing a transparent phonograph record of minutes, blockchain engineering enables participant in a web to verify the genuineness and unity of information. This eliminates the demand for mediator and reduces the potentiality for imposter or use. Blockchain's transparency empower person with control condition over their own information, giving them the power to portion or revoke entrée as desired. This has important deduction for privateers and information protective covering, allowing person to have greater control condition over their personal info. It is essential to note that transparency in blockchain does not equate to complete public nimbleness. While all minutes recorded on a blockchain are transparent, the identity of the participant can be kept anonymous through the usage of pseudonym. This pseudonym preserves privateers while maintaining transparency and protection. Quantum computer science, with its immense computational powerless, also presents opportunity for enhanced transparency. Quantum computing leverages the principle of quantum mechanism to perform calculation that are currently infeasible for classical computer. This opens up new possibility in various fields, including cryptanalysis, optimization, and material scientific discipline. The powerless of quantum computing also comes with the dispute of maintaining transparency and protection in its trading operations. Quantum computer can perform certain calculation exponentially faster than classical computer, which has important deduction for cryptanalysis. Traditional encoding algorithm that rely on the trouble of factoring large Numbers become vulnerable to attack from quantum computer, thereby compromising the protection and privateers of sensitive info. To ensure transparency and protection in the quantum computing epoch, new cryptographic algorithm and protocol known as post-quantum cryptanalysis (PQC) are being developed. PQC aims to provide encoding method that are resistant to attack from both classical and quantum computer, ensuring the confidentiality and unity of info. By implementing PQC, organization and person can prepare for the post-quantum epoch while maintaining transparency and protection in their trading operations. In decision, transparency plays a crucial function in the execution of emerging technology such as artificial intelligence service, blockchain, and quantum computer science. In the instance of AI, attempt are being made to enhance transparency through explainable AI technique that provide penetration into the decision-making procedure. Blockchain engineering offer inherent transparency through its distributed Leger, enabling reliance, answerability, and individual control condition over information. Similarly, in the quantum computing epoch, transparency and protection are maintained through the evolution of post-quantum cryptanalysis. By addressing the challenge associated with transparency, this technology can be harnessed to their full potentiality, creating a hereafter where reliance, equity, and answerability are overriding.

SECURITY

Protection is a critical care when it comes to the sphere of artificial intelligence service, blockchain, and quantum computer science. With the rapid promotion in this technology, there is an increasing demand for robust protection measure to be put in topographic point to protect sensitive information and forestall unauthorized entrée. AI service system, particularly those that involve simple machine acquisition algorithm, are susceptible to various protection hazard. Malicious actor can exploit vulnerability in this system to manipulate the algorithm, leading to biased or misleading consequence. This can have significant deduction, especially in area such as health care and finance, where decision based on AI algorithm can have profound consequence. Ensuring the unity and dependability of AI system is crucial to maintaining the reliance and assurance of user. Similarly, blockchain engineering, which underlies cryptocurrencies like Bitcoin, also faces protection challenge. While blockchain is often touted as procure due to its decentralized and immutable nature, it is not immune to attack. One of the primary concern is the menace of 51 % attack, where a single entity addition control condition of the bulk of the web's computing powerless, enabling them to manipulate minutes and double-spend coin. This poses a significant hazard to the unity and reliance that are fundamental to the blockchain's military operation. Bug and vulnerability in the smart contract that run on blockchain platform can be exploited by hacker to steal finances or pull strings information. It is crucial to develop robust protection mechanism to mitigate these hazard and ensure the continued acceptance and usage of blockchain engineering. Quantum computer science, while promising tremendous computational powerless, also poses protection challenge. Quantum computer have the potential to break the widely-used cryptographic algorithm that currently secure our digital communication theory and minutes. This could lead to the via media of sensitive info, such as personal information, financial minutes, and national protection secret. To address this menace, research worker are working on developing quantum-resistant cryptographic algorithms that can withstand attack from quantum computer. Quantum technology can also be used to enhance protection, such as in the battlefield of quantum key statistical distribution (QKD), which enables procure communicating through the transmittal of quantum-encrypted key. Nonetheless, it is clear that protection in the historic period of quantum computing requires constant invention and version to stay ahead of potential menace. To tackle the protection challenges in artificial intelligence service, blockchain, and quantum computer science, there are several approaches that can be taken. Firstly, investing in inquiry and evolution to identify and address vulnerability is crucial. This requires coaction between academician, manufacture expert, and policymakers to stay abreast of emerging menace and develop countermeasure. Incorporating protection feature into the designing stage of this technology is essential. By considering protection as an integral portion of the evolution procedure, vulnerability can be mitigated before they are exploited. The execution of robust hallmark and entrée control condition system is vital to ensure that only authorized user can interact with this technology. This involves employing multifactor hallmark, encoding, and procure protocol to prevent unauthorized entrée and information breach. Regular audit and monitor of system is also necessary to detect any anomaly or suspicious activity promptly. Organization should invest in robust incidental reaction plan and mechanism to ensure a Swift and effective reaction in the case of a protection rupture. Public consciousness and instruction play a crucial function in enhancing protection. User need to be informed about the hazard associated with this technology and their function in protecting their information and privateers. This can be achieved through educational political campaign, workshop, and training plan that equip person with the cognition and skill to navigate the digital landscape painting safely. In decision, protection is an overriding care in the sphere of artificial intelligence service, blockchain, and quantum computer science. As this technology continue to advance and reshape various industry, it is imperative to address the protection challenges they present. By investing in inquiry, incorporating protection feature, implementing robust hallmark and entrée control condition system, and fostering public consciousness and instruction, we can build a procured and trustworthy ecosystem for the hereafter. Only through these collective attempt can the full potentiality of artificial intelligence service, blockchain, and quantum computing be realized while mitigating the associated hazard.

USE CASES OF BLOCKCHAIN

The debut of blockchain engineering has opened up numerous possibility and potential usage case across various industry. One of the key area where blockchain has found significant practical application is in provision concatenation direction. Due to its inherent feature such as immutableness, decentralization, and transparency, blockchain provides a procure and efficient chemical mechanism for tracking and authenticating the motion of good from their beginning to the terminal consumer. By implementing blockchain in provision concatenation direction, company can ensure the variability and unity of their merchandise, observe and forestall forgery good, and streamline procedure such as stock list direction and logistics. Another manufacture that has shown great involvement in adopting blockchain engineering is finance. Blockchain has the potential to revolutionize the financial manufacture by offering more procure, crystalline, and efficient solution for various financial minutes. For illustration, blockchain can be used to facilitate cross-border payment, eliminating mediator and reducing dealing cost. Blockchain-based smart contract enable programmable and self-executing agreement, automating procedure such as loaning, policy, and plus direction. The decentralized nature of blockchain also enhances protection and reduces the hazard of imposter and information use. Blockchain engineering has also found application in the health care sphere. By leveraging blockchain, healthcare supplier can improve information unity, privateers, interoperability, and entrée control condition. With blockchain-based system, affected role record and medical info can be securely stored and shared across health care supplier, ensuring truth and eliminating extra record. This not only enhances patient attention but also enables research worker and policymakers to entrée comprehensive and reliable information for analytic thinking and decision-making. Blockchain can be used to track the genuineness and provision concatenation of pharmaceutical merchandise, reducing the hazard of forgery drug infiltrating the marketplace and putting patient at hazard. In add-on to this mainstream industry, blockchain engineering has also demonstrated its potential in unconventional area such as voting system and intellectual belongings right direction. By implementing blockchain in voting system, government can enhance the unity and transparency of election, preventing imposter and ensuring accurate consequence. Blockchain can also be used to establish digital identity, enabling person to prove their personal identity without the demand for mediator. In footing of intellectual belongings right direction, blockchain offer a decentralized and immutable political platform for registering and protecting copyright, patent, and hallmark, eliminating the demand for third-party mediator and reducing cost. Blockchain engineering has the potential to revolutionize the free energy sphere by enabling peer-to-peer free energy trade and incentivizing renewable free energy coevals. With blockchain, person and organization can trade excess free energy directly with each other, eliminating the demand for traditional free energy supplier and reducing cost. This not only promotes free energy independence but also encourages the acceptance of renewable free energy beginning, ultimately contributing to a more sustainable hereafter. Blockchain's potential extends beyond traditional computing environment. The outgrowth of blockchain engineering has led to the evolution of decentralized application (Apps) and decentralized autonomous organization (DAOs) . This application leverage the decentralized nature of blockchain to operate without the demand for a central authorization, offering increased transparency and protection. For illustration, Apps can be used to create decentralized market, where user can buy and sell good directly, without the demand for mediator. DAOs, on the other minus, enable decentralized decision-making and administration structure, allowing participant to vote on important matter and collectively manage resource and trading operations. The usage case of blockchain are diverse and continue to diversify as the engineering evolves. From provision concatenation direction to finance, healthcare, voting system, intellectual belongings right direction, free energy, and decentralized application, blockchain has the potential to transform various industry by enhancing protection, transparency, efficiency, and reliance. It is important to note that despite its numerous advantage, blockchain engineering also presents challenge such as scalability, free energy ingestion, and regulatory concern. As the engineering matures, addressing these challenge and exploring new application will be crucial to fully realizing the potentiality of blockchain in shaping the hereafter of our digital club.

CRYPTOCURRENCIES

This have been a groundbreaking invention in the universe of finance and engineering. This digital currency, such as Bitcoin and Ethereum, have revolutionized the manner we think about and use money. One of the main advantage of cryptocurrencies is their decentralized nature, as they are not controlled by any central authorization or authorities. This has allowed for a greater grade of financial exemption and independence, particularly in region with unstable or oppressive political system. Cryptocurrencies have the potentiality to eliminate the demand for mediator, such as Banks, in financial minutes. This can reduce dealing cost and increase efficiency in the global economic system. Cryptocurrencies have the potential to provide financial service to the unbanked and under banked population, who may not have entrée to traditional bank service. As cryptocurrencies become more widely adopted, they have the potential to bring financial comprehension to a million of citizenry around the universe. There are also significant challenge and hazard associated with cryptocurrencies. One major care is their unpredictability, as the economic value of cryptocurrencies can fluctuate significantly in short time period of clip. This makes them a highly risky investing and raises question about their power to serve as a stable shop of economic value. Cryptocurrencies have been associated with illicit activity such as money wash and the funding of act of terrorism, due to the pseudonymous nature of minutes. This has led to concern about the potentiality for cryptocurrencies to be used for illegal purpose and has prompted increased regulatory examination. Another dispute is the scalability of cryptocurrencies, as the current blockchain engineering that underpins them can only handle a limited figure of minutes per sec. This has led to issue with web over-crowding and dealing delay, particularly during time period of high requirement. There are also concern about the environmental wallop of cryptocurrencies, particularly Bitcoin, as the excavation procedure requires a significant sum of computational powerless and free energy ingestion. Despite these challenge, cryptocurrencies have the potential to reshape the global financial scheme and democratize entrée to financial service. The underlying blockchain engineering that power cryptocurrencies also has broader application beyond finance. Blockchain is a distributed Leger that allows for procure and transparent record-keeping of minutes. It has the potential to revolutionize industry such as provision concatenation direction, health care, and voting system. For illustration, blockchain can be used to verify the genuineness and birthplace of good, ensuring that consumer has entrée to accurate info about the merchandise they purchase. In health care, blockchain can facilitate the procure communion of affected role information, enabling more efficient and personalized health care service. In the linguistic context of voting system, blockchain can provide a procure and crystalline method acting for conducting election, reducing the hazard of imposter and use. The convergence of AI, blockchain, and quantum computer science has the potential to drive even greater invention and transmutation. AI can enhance the capability of blockchain by automating procedure and providing real-time penetration from the vast sum of information generated by blockchain network. Quantum computer science, on the other minus, can increase the protection and efficiency of blockchain by improving encoding and speeding up complex calculation. The combining of this technology has the potential to unlock new possibility in area such as finance, health care, and cybersecurity. In decision, cryptocurrencies have transformed the financial landscape painting and offer the potential to bring financial comprehension to a million of citizenry around the universe. While there are challenge and hazard associated with cryptocurrencies, their underlying blockchain engineering has broader application beyond finance. The convergence of AI, blockchain, and quantum computer science has the potential to drive even greater invention and transmute various industry. As this technology continue to evolve, it is crucial to strike a proportion between invention and ordinance to ensure the responsible and inclusive deployment of this technology.

SUPPLY CHAIN MANAGEMENT

Supply concatenation direction is a critical facet of business in nowadays's globalized economic system. It involves the coordination and integrating of various activity, procedure, and stakeholder to ensure the efficient flowing of good and service from the detail of beginning to the detail of ingestion. The aim of provision concatenation direction is to optimize the entire provision concatenation web in footing of monetary value, velocity, caliber, and feebleness. The coming of AI, blockchain engineering, and quantum computer science has significantly impacted provision concatenation direction practice. AI technology, such as simple machine acquisition and predictive analytics, have improved the decision-making procedure by analyzing large volume of information and providing penetration for prediction, stock list direction, requirement preparation, and hazard appraisal. For illustration, AI-powered algorithm can analyze historical gross sales information, marketplace tendency, and external factor to generate accurate requirement prognosis, reducing stock outs and excess stock list. AI can enable the mechanization of provision concatenation procedure, enhancing productiveness and reducing cost. For case, autonomous vehicle equipped with AI algorithm can optimize path preparation, programming, and fire ingestion, resulting in fast and more efficient delivery. Similarly, AI-powered automaton and drone can automate repetitive undertaking in warehouse, improving order of magnitude fulfillment and reducing labor cost. AI can assist in caliber direction by analyzing information from detector and camera to identify defect or deviation from caliber standard, enabling real-time corrective action. Blockchain engineering has also emerged as a transformative instrument for enhancing transparency, traceability, and reliance in provision irons. It is a distributed Leger engineering that enables to procure, immutable, and decentralized transcription of minutes. By leveraging blockchain, organization can create a tamper-proof phonograph record of every dealing, from the source of raw material to the bringing of the final merchandise, ensuring transparency and answerability. This can be particularly useful in industry where birthplace and genuineness are critical, such as nutrient and pharmaceutical. Blockchain can also enable better provision concatenation coaction by providing a shared political platform for multiple stakeholder, including supplier, manufacturer, distributor, and customer. By sharing relevant information, such as stock list degree, product capacity, and requirement prognosis, participant can make more informed decision, improve coordination, and reduce lead multiplication. Blockchain can also facilitate the execution of smart contract, which are self-executing contract with predefined rule and weather. This can eliminate the demand for mediator and streamline defrayal procedure, reducing dealing cost and enhancing efficiency. Another emerging engineering that holds great hope for provision concatenation direction is quantum computing. Quantum computing utilizes quantum natural philosophy principle to perform complex calculation that are beyond the capability of classical computer. This can enable provision concatenation optimization, such as solving the traveling salesman job, which involves finding the shortest path to visit an exercise set of location. By finding an optimal path, provision concatenation cost can be minimized, and bringing multiplication can be reduced. Quantum computer science can also enhance provision concatenation resiliency by simulating various scenarios and identifying vulnerable point on the web. By understanding potential hazard and break, organization can proactively devise eventuality plan and implement extenuation scheme to ensure the persistence of trading operations. Quantum computing can facilitate faster and more accurate requirement prediction, considering various factors, such as seasonality, marketplace tendency, and consumer behavior. This can enable organization to align their product and logistics capacity with anticipated requirement, reducing the hazard of overstocking or stock outs. In decision, the integrating of artificial intelligence service, blockchain engineering, and quantum computer science has revolutionized provision concatenation direction practice. This technology have enabled organization to enhance decision-making, automatize procedure, improve transparency, coaction, and reliance, and optimize provision concatenation trading operations. As business strive to stay competitive and meet the increasing expectation of customer, embracing this technology can provide a significant vantage in the complex and dynamic universe of provision concatenation direction.

VOTING SYSTEMS

Another country where blockchain engineering has the potential to make a significant wallop is in voting system. The current vote system in topographic point around the universe are often criticized for being outdated, susceptible to use, and lacking transparency. Blockchain engineering can address these issue by providing a procured and transparent political platform for conducting election. One of the key advantage of using blockchain engineering in voting system is the protection it offers. Traditional vote system are vulnerable to imposter, meddling, and chop. By storing vote on a decentralized blockchain web, it becomes nearly impossible for anyone to alter or manipulate the information. Each ballot is recorded in a city block, encrypted, and linked to the previous city block, creating an immutable and transparent Leger of vote. This ensures the unity of the vote procedure and instills reliance in the final result. Another welfare of using blockchain in voting system is the addition in transparency. In traditional vote system, the procedure of count and tallying vote can be opaque, leading to doubt and intuition.

Blockchain engineering, on the other minus, provides a public and transparent phonograph record of each ballot, allowing voter and perceived to independently verify the consequence. This increased transparency can help to build assurance in the electoral procedure and reduce dispute over the cogency of the result. Blockchain engineering can also address issue of handiness and inclusivity in vote. In many state, citizen face barrier when it comes to participating in election, such as physical disability, geographical placement, or deficiency of designation. Blockchain-based voting system can overcome this barrier by allowing citizen to vote remotely using their digital identity, ensuring that everyone has an equal chance to participate in the democratic procedure. The usage of blockchain can also prevent elector imposter by verifying the personal identity of each elector and ensuring that they are eligible to cast their vote. Despite the potential benefit, there are still challenge and consideration that need to be addressed when implementing blockchain-based vote system. One major care is the privateers of voter. While blockchain ensures the protection and transparency of the vote, it also raises question about privateers and the confidentiality of the information. It is important to strike a proportion between transparency and privateers to protect the identity of individual voter while still maintaining the unity of the overall scheme. Another dispute is the scalability of the blockchain web. As the figure of participant and minutes addition, the blockchain web may experience over-crowding and slower process multiplication. This could potentially limit the efficiency of the vote procedure and make delay in the bringing of consequence. Scalability solution, such as layer-2 protocol or sharing, need to be explored to overcome these restriction and ensure that blockchain-based vote system can handle large-scale election effectively. There is also the number of reliance in the engineering itself. Blockchain engineering is still relatively new and not widely understood by the general populace. There may be incredulity and opposition towards adopting blockchain-based vote system due to strangeness with the engineering or concern about chop and protection vulnerability. Education and transparency political campaign will be crucial in building reliance and credence of blockchain as a reliable and secure answer for voting system. In decision, blockchain engineering holds tremendous potentiality in transforming voting system to be more procure, crystalline, and inclusive. By leveraging blockchain's protection and transparency feature, the unity of election can be enhanced, and reliance in the electoral procedure can be restored. Challenge related to privateers, scalability, and trust need to be carefully addressed to ensure the successful execution of blockchain-based vote system. As the engineering continues to evolve, further inquiry and evolution are needed to optimize and refine the usage of blockchain in vote and pave the manner for a more democratic and participatory club.

POTENTIAL BENEFITS AND CHALLENGES OF BLOCKCHAIN

Potential benefit and challenge of blockchain engineering holds immense potentiality for various sectors, presenting numerous benefit as well as certain challenge. One of the significant advantage is its power to enhance transparency and protection in minutes. The decentralized nature of blockchain guarantee that all participant have entrée to a shared Leger, enabling real-time and immutable update. This degree of transparency can greatly reduce imposter, as tampering with information would require altering all subsequent block, thus making it highly impractical and easily detectable. The cryptographic algorithm employed in blockchain ensure the protection of minutes, making it nearly impossible for hacker to manipulate or entrée sensitive info. These feature render blockchain an ideal answer for industry such as finance, where reliance and protection are overriding. Another potential welfare of blockchain engineering lies in its potential to streamline and automate procedure, thereby increasing efficiency and reducing cost. Traditional record-keeping system often involves complex and time-consuming paperwork, prostrate to human mistake. In direct contrast, blockchain provides a decentralized and immutable database that eliminates the demand for mediator, significantly reducing the bureaucratism associated with record-keeping. For case, in the provision concatenation manufacture, blockchain facilitates the trailing of good from their beginning to their final finish in a

121

crystalline and procure mode, reducing delay, mistake, and ultimately, cost. Similarly, the usage of blockchain in smart contract can automate contractual procedure, ensuring that footing and weather are met without the demand for mediator or legal system. These advantage can revolutionize industry, leading to increased efficiency and productiveness. Blockchain can foster reliance and coaction among various stakeholders, particularly in industry involving complex provision irons or multi-party minutes. By allowing multiple entity to entrée and lend to a common Leger, blockchain engineering reduces the inherent misgiving between participant. In the health care sphere, where affected role information is often fragmented across various system, blockchain can enable procure and interoperable communion of medical record, allowing healthcare supplier to make informed decision and deliver better affected role attention. Similarly, in the battlefield of intellectual belongings, blockchain can facilitate the enrollment and protective covering of copyright, hallmark, and patent, thereby promoting invention and coaction. The enhanced reliance and coaction offered by blockchain have the potentiality to transform various industry, fostering new concern model and accelerating growing. While the potential benefit of blockchain are substantial, several challenges must be addressed for its widespread acceptance. One of the main challenge is scalability. As the figure of minutes addition, the sizing of the blockchain grows exponentially, reducing the efficiency of the scheme. To overcome this dispute, various solution, such as the execution of off-chain minutes or the usage of sharing technique, are being explored. The free energy ingestion associated with blockchain minutes, particularly in the instance of proof-of-work consensus mechanism, raises concern about sustainability. It is imperative to develop alternative consensus mechanism that are less energy-intensive, to ensure the long-term viability of blockchain engineering. Another dispute is the regulatory environs surrounding blockchain. The decentralized nature of blockchain limit the control condition and inadvertence of centralized regulatory body, posing legal and conformity challenge. The cross-border nature of blockchain minutes complicates the enforcement of regulation, requiring international cooperation and standardization. Government and regulatory body need to establish clear model and guideline to address these challenge, ensuring the responsible and secure usage of blockchain engineering. The trust on cryptographic algorithm in blockchain introduce vulnerability to cyberattack. Although blockchain is designed to be secure, there have been case of hacker exploiting failing in the underlying cryptographic algorithm or the execution of smart contract. Addressing this vulnerability requires continuous inquiry and updates to ensure the hardiness and unity of blockchain system. As blockchain involves the direction of significant sum of information, privateers concern arise. Balancing the demand for transparency and privateers is a significant dispute that must be addressed to build public reliance in blockchain engineering. In decision, blockchain engineering offers numerous benefit, ranging from transparency and protection to increased efficiency and coaction. Challenge such as scalability, free energy ingestion, regulatory model, cyber vulnerability, and privateers concern need to be overcome for its widespread acceptance. As technological promotion continue, it is crucial to address these challenge and capitalize on the potentiality of blockchain in various sectors, thus paving the manner for a hereafter of procure, effective, and trusted minutes.

DATA INTEGRITY

Data unity mention to the truth, consistence, and dependability of information stored and processed in various computing machine system. In the linguistic context of AI, blockchain, and quantum computer science, ensuring information unity becomes overriding due to the potential hazard and complexity associated with this technology. AI, with its power to gather and analyze large volume of information, heavily relies on information unity to make accurate prediction and decision. Similarly, blockchain engineering, with its decentralized nature and immutableness, trust on information unity to ensure the cogency and transparency of minutes recorded on the blockchain. Quantum computer science, with its immense computational powerless, poses challenge to information unity as it can potentially break commonly used encoding scheme, putting sensitive information at hazard. In the kingdom of AI, information unity plays a pivotal function in the effectivity and dependability of simple machine learning algorithm. Machine learning algorithms rely on vast sum of information to train model and make accurate prediction. If the input signal information is compromised or lacks unity, the end product consequence of this algorithm can be misleading or even harmful. For case, consider a simple machine learning algorithmic rule used for medical diagnosing. If the preparation information is filled with erroneous or incomplete medical record, the algorithmic rule may learn wrong form and provide inaccurate diagnosis. This highlights the demand for ensuring information unity in AI system through technique such as information proof, information cleaning, and auditing to prevent bias and inaccuracy in the acquisition procedure. Blockchain engineering, known for its decentralized and tamper-proof nature, heavily relies on information unity to maintain the reliance of its user. In a blockchain web, each dealing is recorded in a city block, and this block are linked together using cryptographic hash, forming an immutable concatenation of record. Data unity is ensured by the consensus chemical mechanism employed by the blockchain web, which requires the bulk of participant to agree on the cogency of each dealing before it can be added to the concatenation. This decentralized consensus chemical mechanism and the immutableness of the blockchain make it near impossible to alter or manipulate the recorded information, maintaining its unity and genuineness. Achieving information unity in blockchain network goes beyond the immutableness of the information itself. It also involves verifying the information inputted into the scheme, ensuring that the information being recorded is accurate and reliable. This can be achieved through various mechanism such as information proof and digital signature. Data proof technique help ensure that the info being recorded on the blockchain is in the correct formatting and adhere to predefined rule and standard. Digital signature, on the other minus, provide an agency of verifying the genuineness and unity of the information. By digitally signing minutes using cryptographic algorithm, participant can prove the possession and unity of the information they submit to the blockchain web. Quantum computer science, with its immense computational powerless, brings new challenge and concern regarding information unity. Quantum computer have the potential to break

126

commonly used encoding algorithm, compromising the confidentiality and unity of sensitive information. As quantum computer become more powerful, traditional encoding method may no longer be sufficient to protect information from malicious attack. Ensuring information unity in the historic period of quantum computing requires the evolution of quantum-resistant encoding scheme and post-quantum cryptanalysis. These cryptographic technique aim to withstand the computational powerless of quantum computer and provide long-term information unity and protection. In decision, information unity is crucial in the kingdom of AI, blockchain, and quantum computing to ensure accurate prediction, maintain reliance in blockchain network, and protect sensitive info from quantum attack. Achieving information unity involves technique such as information proof, information cleaning, auditing in AI, consensus mechanism and digital signature in blockchain, and quantum-resistant encoding scheme in the epoch of quantum computer science. By prioritizing information unity and implementing robust measure to ensure its truth, dependability, and consistence, we can harness the full potentiality of this technology while maintaining the reliance and protection of our digital universe.

REDUCED INTERMEDIARIES

Reduced mediator is another significant vantage that arises from the integrating of artificial intelligence service, blockchain, and quantum computer science. Traditional mediator, such as Banks, agent, and lawyer, play a crucial function in facilitating various minutes and enforcing agreement. Their engagement often leads to delays, increased cost, and potential hazard associated with human mistake. With the execution of these advanced technology, the demand for mediator decrease significantly, resulting in a streamlined and efficient procedure. Firstly, artificial intelligence service can revolutionize the financial sphere by reducing the essential for Banks and agent. AI-powered algorithm can autonomously analyze vast sum of information, allowing for real-time decision-making and accurate prediction. This eliminates the demand for a human agent who may introduce prejudice or inefficiency into the trade procedure. Smart contract powered by AI can automate and enforce agreement, reducing the trust on Banks for escrow service. This not only speeds up minutes but also provides a more procure and crystalline chemical mechanism for carrying out financial interaction. Blockchain engineering further extinguish mediator by creating a decentralized and secure scheme for recording and verifying minutes. Traditionally, mediator such as Banks and lawyer are required to provide edibleness and hallmark to various minutes. With blockchain, every dealing is securely stored in a distributed Leger that is transparent and tamper-proof. This

129

eliminates the demand for mediator to guarantee the genuineness of minutes, as the blockchain itself provides this self-assurance. As a consequence, blockchain engineering reduce cost, improves efficiency, and increases reliance among participant, ultimately rendering mediator redundant in many scenarios. Quantum computer science has the potential to revolutionize information protection and privateers, which are traditionally maintained by mediator such as encoding service and government. Quantum computer, with their exponentially higher computational powerless, can crack currently unbreakable encoding code, putting sensitive info at hazard. Quantum computing can also offer an answer to this job by providing enforceable cryptographic system. With quantum encoding, info can be securely transmitted and stored without the demand for mediator to ensure confidentiality. This eliminates the potential vulnerability introduced by mediator and reduces the hazard of information breach and unauthorized entrée. Quantum computing can enhance privateers by enabling zero-knowledge proof, a cryptographic conception that allows party to validate the genuineness of their statement without revealing any sensitive info. This means that person can prove possession or making without disclosing specific inside information, protecting their privateers while still ensuring reliance among participant. This engineering has vast deduction beyond individual privateers, as it can be applied in various industry, including health care and finance, where mediator often handle sensitive information and personal info. The integrating of artificial intelligence service, blockchain, and quantum computing lead to a significant decrease in mediator across various industry. By utilizing AI algorithm and smart contract, business can automate and streamline minutes, reducing the trust on Banks and agent. Blockchain engineering eliminates the demand for mediator to authenticate minutes, providing a trusted and secure environs for participant. Quantum computing offer advanced cryptographic system that enhance information protection and privateers, rendering mediator such as encoding service unnecessary. The riddance of mediator through the execution of these advanced technology not only leads to cost nest egg and increased efficiency but also Foster transparency, reliance, and privateers in various sectors of the economic system. As this technology continue to evolve and mature, their wallop on reducing mediator is expected to grow even further, paving the manner for a more decentralized and streamlined hereafter.

SCALABILITY ISSUES

Scalability issue are a critical care in the fields of AI, blockchain, and quantum computer science. As this technology continue to advance and permeate various industry, the demand to handle vast sum of information and calculation become increasingly apparent. In AI, scalability issue arise when system is unable to efficiently process large datasets or handle a growing figure of user concurrently. This can hinder the public presentation and effectivity of AI algorithm, leading to slower reaction multiplication and decreased truth. In the linguistic context of blockchain, scalability issue arise due to the decentralized nature of the engineering. As more minutes are added to the blockchain, the web can become congested, resulting in longer verification multiplication and increased dealing fee. The sizing of the blockchain itself continues to grow, making it increasingly difficult for new node to join the web or maintain a complete transcript of the Leger. In quantum computer science, scalability issue stem from the complex and delicate nature of quantum system. Quantum computer are highly sensitive to environmental perturbation, making it challenging to scale up their architecture while maintaining the necessary degree of staleness and coherency. Quantum algorithm often requires an exponential figure of qubits to solve certain problem, posing significant ironware challenge due to the fragile nature of qubits. Scalability issue are a pressing care in these emerging fields, and addressing them will be essential for the widespread acceptance and promotion of AI, blockchain, and quantum computing technology.

The potentiality for the integrating of AI, blockchain engineering, and quantum computer science is one that holds immense hope for the hereafter. As the capability and application of AI continue to expand, the demand for more procure and transparent system becomes increasingly apparent. Blockchain engineering, with its decentralized and immutable nature, offers a potential answer to this protection and transparency concern. By incorporating AI into blockchain system, more efficient and intelligent decision-making procedure can be implemented, further enhancing the overall functionality and effectivity of such system. One country where the integrating of AI and blockchain engineering can have a significant wallop is in provision concatenation direction. Supply irons are often complex network involving multiple party and procedure, making it challenging to track and verify each dealing or fundamental interaction. This complexes can lead to inefficiency, delay, and increased cost. Blockchain engineering can provide a crystalline and immutable Leger that records all minutes and interaction in real-time, allowing for easier traceability and answerability. The swerve bulk of information generated within provision irons can be overwhelming, making it difficult for world to analyze and extract meaningful penetration. This is where AI comes in. AI algorithm can analyze the vast sum of information stored on the blockchain and place form, tendency, and anomaly. By applying simple machine learning technique, AI can learn from past information and make prediction or recommendation, improving the efficiency, truth, and effectivity of decision-making procedure. For case, AI can help identify potential constriction or area of betterment within the provision concatenation, leading to proactive measure and more streamlined trading operations. Another country where the integrating of AI and blockchain engineering can have a transformative consequence is in the health care manufacture. The health care sphere generates vast sum of sensitive affected role information, which must be securely stored, shared, and accessed by authorized party. Traditional centralized storehouse system are vulnerable to data breach and hacking attempt, compromising patient privateers and protection. Blockchain engineering can decentralize and distribute the storehouse of affected role information, ensuring that no single entity has complete control condition over the information. The usage of smart contract on the blockchain can automate and streamline administrative procedure, reducing cost and improving efficiency. As AI is applied to healthcare information stored on the blockchain, immense possibility emerge. AI algorithm can analyze patient information to identify form, detect early sign of disease, and predict intervention result. This can lead to more precise and personalized health care intervention, improving patient result and reducing health care cost. AI can aid in medical inquiry by analyzing vast sum of affected role information to identify tendency or correlation that may lead to new penetration or intervention discovery. The integrating of AI and blockchain engineering in health care has the potential to revolutionize the manufacture and transform the manner health care is delivered and managed. The integrating of quantum computing with AI and blockchain engineering opens up even more possibility for invention and promotion. Quantum computer science, with its power to process vast sum of information in analogue, can significantly enhance the computational powerless of AI algorithm. This can lead to more sophisticated and accurate AI model, ca-

135

pable of handling complex problem that would otherwise be intractable with classical computer science. Quantum cryptanalysis, a subfield of quantum computer science, can address the protection concern of blockchain engineering. Quantum cryptographic system leverage the principle of quantum mechanism to provide provably secure communicating channel. This can potentially eliminate the vulnerability of traditional cryptographic system and provide an even higher degree of protection for blockchain network. In decision, the integrating of AI, blockchain engineering, and quantum computing holds immense hope for the hereafter. The potential application is far-reaching, from enhancing provision concatenation direction and revolutionizing health care to providing unparalleled degree of protection and privateers in blockchain network. As this technology continue to evolve and mature, it is crucial for research worker, developer, and policymakers to collaborate and ensure the responsible and ethical execution of this technology. With careful circumstance and proactive measure, the integrating of AI, blockchain engineering, and quantum computing can truly transform industry and drive invention in the old age to come.

IV. QUANTUM COMPUTING

Quantum computer science quantum computer science has emerged as a promising battlefield that has the potential to revolutionize various aspects of scientific discipline, engineering, and even club as a unit. Unlike classical computer that rely on binary digit or spot, quantum computer utilize qubits, which can exist in a principle of superposition of state, thanks to the principle of quantum mechanism. These belonging allows quantum computer to handle complex calculation at an unprecedented velocity and efficiency, potentially solving problem that are currently considered intractable for classical computer. The powerless of quantum computing lie in its power to harness the unique property of quantum mechanism, such as web and principle of superposition, to perform calculation. Entanglement mention to the phenomenon where two or more qubits become interconnected, so that the province of one qubit affects the province of the other qubits, regardless of the length between them. These belonging enables quantum computer to perform parallel calculation and procedure vast sum of info simultaneously, leading to a significant acceleration in solving certain problem, such as factoring large Numbers or simulating quantum system. Superposition, on the other minus, allows qubits to exist in multiple state simultaneously. This means that while a classical spot can only represent either a 0 or a 1, a qubit can represent a combining of 0 and 1, known as a quantum principle of superposition. By manipulating and measuring qubits in a principle of superposition, quantum computer can explore multiple possibility simultaneously and arrive at the optimal answer much faster than classical computer through a procedure known as quantum correspondence. Despite the promising potentiality of quantum computer science, the battlefield is still in its early phase and faces numerous challenge. One of the major obstacle is the number of qubit staleness and decoherence. Quits are highly sensitive to environmental dissonance and perturbation, which can cause them to lose their quantum property and prostration into classical spot. This makes it extremely difficult to maintain the unity of quantum info over long time period of clip, hindering the practicality and scalability of quantum computing system. Research worker are actively exploring various method to mitigate decoherence, such as mistake rectification code and different qubit architecture, to enhance the staleness and dependability of qubits. Another dispute in quantum computer science is the deficiency of a universal quantum computing machine, capable of performing a wide scope of undertaking. Currently, most quantum computer are limited to specific trading operations and are not versatile enough to handle complex calculation. This is primarily due to the trouble in achieving and maintaining the necessary degree of qubit coherency and control condition, as well as the deficiency of mistake rectification mechanism. Significant advancement has been made in recent old age, with the evolution of quantum annealed and gate-model quantum computer that can perform more versatile undertaking. It is still an ongoing inquiry country to develop a scalable and fault-tolerant linguistic universal quantum computing machine that can surpass the capability of classical computer. Despite these challenge, quantum computer science has the potential to revolutionize various fields. One of the most promising application of quantum computer science is in cryptanalysis. Quantum computer have the power to break many of the normally used public-key encoding algorithm by exploiting their enhanced computational powerless, posing a significant menace to the protection of sensitive information. Quantum computer science also offers potential solution to this job through the evolution of quantum-resistant encoding algorithms that are resilient to quantum attack. In add-on to cryptanalysis, quantum computing can also have a profound wallop on optimization problem, computer simulation of complex system, dose find, and simple machine acquisition. Due to the exponential acceleration provided by quantum correspondence, quantum computer can efficiently solve optimization problem that are crucial in various spheres, such as logistics, finance, and provision concatenation direction. Quantum computer can simulate the behavior of quantum system with a high degree of truth, enabling scientist to study and understand complex quantum phenomenon that are currently beyond the range of classical computer. This opens up new possibility for the geographic expedition of material, drug, and chemical reaction. Quantum computing can also enhance simple machine learning algorithm by providing more efficient method for process and analyzing big information. Quantum simple machine learning algorithm have the potentiality to transform various sectors, such as health care, finance, and transportation system, by enabling faster and more accurate prediction and decision-making procedure. In decision, quantum computing holds tremendous hope for revolutionizing various aspects of scientific discipline, engineering, and club. The unique property of quantum mechanism, such as web and principle of superposition, enable quantum computer to perform complex calculation at an unprecedented velocity and efficiency. There are still significant challenge to overcome, such as qubit staleness and the deficiency of a universal quantum computing machine. Nonetheless, the potential application of quantum computing in cryptanalysis, optimization, computer simulation, dose find, and simple machine learning make it an exciting and rapidly evolving battlefield with the potential to reshape the hereafter.

OVERVIEW OF QUANTUM COMPUTING

Quantum computing represents a paradigm displacement in the battlefield of computing machine scientific discipline. Unlike classical computer that operate using spot, which can represent either a 0 or a 1, quantum computer utilize qubits, which can exist in a principle of superposition of both state simultaneously. This enables them to perform calculation in analogue and exponentially increase their process powerless. In add-on to the principle of superposition rule, quantum computer also exploit the conception of web, whereby the state of multiple qubits become correlated and interdependent on each other. This unique property of quantum computing have the potential to revolutionize various fields, including cryptanalysis, optimization, and simple machine acquisition. One of the most significant application of quantum computer science is in the battlefield of cryptanalysis. With the coming of powerful classical computer, many encoding schemes that were once considered procure are now vulnerable to brute forcefulness attack. Quantum computer have the power to break these encoding scheme by utilizing algorithm such as Shor's algorithmic rule, which can efficiently factor large Numbers. This poses a significant menace to the protection of current communicating system and digital minutes. Quantum computing can also provide solution to this job through the evolution of quantum-resistant encoding algorithm, such as lattice-based cryptanalysis and multivariate cryptanalysis. These algorithms purchase the computational complexes of certain mathematical problem to provide robust protection against both classical and quantum attack. Quantum key statistical distribution (QKD) protocol, such as the BB84 communications protocol, can enable secure communicating by leveraging the principle of quantum mechanism to detect any listen in attempt. By integrating quantum computing into the battlefield of cryptanalysis, it is possible to both enhance protection and address the vulnerability imposed by quantum computer. Another battlefield that stands to benefit from quantum computer science is optimization. Many real-world problem, such as programming, logistics, and resourcefulness allotment, involve a large figure of variable and constraint, which make them computationally challenging to solve using classical computer. Quantum computing offers the potentiality to provide more efficient and effective solution to this optimization problem. By applying quantum algorithm, such as the quantum approximate optimization algorithmic rule (AOA) or the quantum annealing algorithmic rule, it becomes possible to explore a larger search infinite of potential solution and identify the optimal or near-optimal answer more quickly. This has important deduction for industry such as transportation system, finance, and provision concatenation direction, where even marginal improvement in efficiency and monetary value can yield significant benefit. Machine acquisition is yet another country that can be revolutionized by quantum computer science. Traditional simple machine acquisition algorithm, such as reinforcement transmitter machine and neural network, often encounter challenge when dealing with large datasets and complex problem. Quantum simple machine acquisition (QML) aims to leverage the unique property of quantum computer to overcome these challenge and unlock new capability in pattern acknowledgment, optimization, and information analytic thinking.

142

Quantum algorithm, such as the quantum reinforcement transmitter simple machine and quantum variational algorithm, have shown hope in addressing these issue and improving the public presentation of simple machine acquisition model. By harnessing the powerless of quantum computer science, it becomes possible to develop more exact and efficient simple machine acquisition model, advancing the capability of artificial intelligence service and opening new opportunity in fields such as dose find, mental image acknowledgment, and natural linguistic communication process. Despite the immense potentiality of quantum computer science, there are significant challenge that must be overcome before its widespread acceptance. One major dispute lies in the evolution of reliable and scalable qubits. Quantum system are highly susceptible to noise and mistake caused by environmental perturbation, which can quickly degrade the public presentation of quantum computer. Error rectification technique, such as quantum mistake rectification code and fault-tolerant quantum computer science, are essential for maintaining the unity and dependability of quantum calculation. Significant promotion in quantum ironware, such as improving qubit coherency and reducing decoherence personal effects, are necessary to build quantum computer capable of solving complex real-world problem. The scalability of quantum algorithm and their integrating with classical computing system are crucial for practical execution. Collaborative attempt from academe, manufacture, and authorities agency are essential to address these challenge and accelerate the evolution and realization of practical quantum computing system. In decision, quantum computing represents a groundbreaking promotion in the battlefield of computing machine scientific discipline. The power to manipulate qubits in principle of superposition and entangle their state offer unprecedented computational powerless and the potential to solve complex problem more efficiently. The application of quantum computing is diverse, ranging from cryptanalysis and optimization to simple machine acquisition. Significant challenge must be overcome before the full potentiality of quantum computer science can be realized. With continued inquiry and technological promotion, quantum computer science has the potential to revolutionize various industry and shape the hereafter of artificial intelligence service, blockchain, and computing as a unit.

KEY PRINCIPLES OF QUANTUM COMPUTING

Key principle of quantum computing quantum computer science is a revolutionary attack to calculation that takes vantage of the principle of quantum mechanism to perform calculation at an unprecedented velocity and efficiency. There are several key principles that underpin the operation of quantum computer, each of which contributes to the immense powerless that this machine posse. First and foremost, quantum computer rely on the fundamental conception of principle of superposition. Unlike classical spot, which can only represent an economic value of 0 or 1, quantum spot, or qubits, can exist in a principle of super-position of both state simultaneously. This means that a qubit can have an economic value of 0 and 1 at the same clip, repre-senting all possible combination of 0s and 1s. These belongings of principle of superposition let quantum computer to perform many calculations in analogue, exponentially increasing their computational powerless compared to classical computer. An-other crucial rule of quantum computer science is entanglement. Web occurs when two or more qubits become linked in such a manner that the province of one qubit is dependent on the prov-ince of another, regardless of the physical length between them. This means that the province of one qubit cannot be described independently of the other qubits with which it is entangled. As a consequence, the use of one qubit can instantaneously affect the province of entangled qubits, even if they are separated by great distance. These belongings of web let quantum computer to perform complex calculation by leveraging the interconnection of qubits and exploiting their core relativity. Quantum computer rely on the conception of quantum intervention. Quantum intervention mention to the phenomenon where the chance amplitude associated with the quantum state of qubits can interfere constructively or destructively, depending on their relative phase. This intervention allows quantum computer to exploit the wave-like nature of quantum system and manipulate qubits to enhance or suppress certain result. By carefully technology the intervention between qubits, quantum computer can amplify the chance of obtaining the correct answer to a calculation while simultaneously reducing the chance of obtaining incorrect solution. The rule of quantum correspondence is fundamental to the operation of quantum computer. Quantum correspondence mention to the power of quantum computer to explore multiple way simultaneously and compute on all possible input signal concurrently rather than sequentially. While classical computer require time-consuming iteration to test all possible combination of input signal, quantum computer can compute the consequence of a given calculation by evaluating all possible input signal concurrently. This correspondence greatly accelerates the velocity at which calculation can be performed, making quantum computer highly efficient in solving complex problem exponentially faster than classical computer. A key rule of quantum computer science is the conception of quantum decoherence. Quantum decoherence mention to the deprivation of quantum coherency in a quantum scheme due to interaction with its environs. When a quantum scheme becomes coherent, its quantum province collapse to a classical province, effectively destroying the delicate quantum info that was being processed. Quantum decoherence poses a significant dispute to the evolution and scalability of quantum computer as it limits the clip during which quantum calculation can be performed accurately. Consequently, extensive attempt are being made to develop error-correction technique and to minimize the personal effects of decoherence in order of magnitude to make quantum computing more reliable and practical. In decision, quantum computer science is founded on an exercise set of key principle that differentiate it from classical computer science and enable its extraordinary computational powerless. The principle of superposition, web, quantum intervention, quantum correspondence, and quantum decoherence piece of work in harmoniousness to facilitate the use and process of quantum info. This principle allow quantum computer to solve complex problem exponentially faster and more efficiently than classical computer, promising discovery in various fields, including cryptanalysis, optimization, and dose find. As our apprehension of quantum mechanism intensify and quantum technology continue to advance, the potentiality of quantum computer science will likely be realized, revolutionizing the capability of artificial intelligence service, blockchain, and many other applications in the hereafter.

SUPERPOSITION

Superposition, the first rule of quantum mechanism, mention to the power of quantum system to exist in multiple state simultaneously. This conception challenges our classical apprehension of world, which states that a physical object can only exist in one province at a clip. In a principle of superposition, an atom can be in a province of both being and not being at the same clip, until it is measured and collapses into a single province. This phenomenon has profound deduction for the battlefield of quantum computer science, as it allows for the parallel process of info. Superposition originate from the wave-particle dichotomy of quantum system. According to quantum hypothesis, atom can exhibit both wave-like and particle-like property. Wave can exist in a scope of state, with each province having a certain chance of being measured. This chance is represented by a wave function, which describes the quantum province of an atom. When a measuring is made, the wave function collapses into one of its possible state, and the atom is observed in a definite province. The conception of principle of superposition was famously illustrated by the double-slit experimentation. In this experimentation, a radio beam of visible light or a watercourse of atom is directed at a roadblock with two slit. Behind the roadblock, a silver screen records the form of atom that pass through the slit. In classical natural philosophy, one would expect to observe two separate set of atom on the silver screen, corresponding to the two slit. In the quantum kingdom, something different happen. When atom are shot individually through the slit, they show an intervention form on the silver screen, as if they were waved. This intervention form is explained by the principle of superposition of multiple state of the atom. Each atom passes through both slit simultaneously, interfering with itself and creating an intervention form on the silver screen. Superposition forms the footing of quantum calculation. Unlike classical spot, which can be in a province of either 0 or 1, quantum spot, or qubits, can exist in a principle of superposition of 0 and This means that a qubit can represent both state at the same clip, allowing for exponentially more computational possibility. For illustration, a scheme of n qubits can represent 2^n state simultaneously, whereas classical spot can only represent one province at a clip. Superposition enable quantum computer to perform complex calculation much faster than classical computer. By using quantum algorithm such as Shor's algorithmic rule for factoring large Numbers, quantum computer have the potential to break current cryptographic system, threatening the protection of digital communicating. The quantum computer simulation of physical system, such as chemical reaction or stuff property, could revolutionize fields such as dose find and material scientific discipline. Principle of superposition is a delicate province that can easily be disrupted by interaction with the environs, a procedure known as decoherence. Decoherence causes the wave function to collapse into a single province, destroying the quantum property of the scheme. This poses a significant dispute for the practical realization of quantum computer, as maintaining the fragile principle of superposition province is crucial for their trading operations. Attempt are being made to overcome the number of decoherence and extend the coherency clip of quantum system. One attack is using error rectification code, similar to those used in classical computer, to protect quantum info from mistake caused by decoherence. Another attack is utilizing topological qubits, which are more robust against decoherence due to their inherent quantum protective covering. In decision, principle of superposition is a fundamental rule of quantum mechanism that allows quantum system to exist in multiple state simultaneously. This conception challenges our classical apprehension of world and forms the footing of quantum computer science. By leveraging the powerless of principle of superposition, quantum computer have the potential to solve complex problem at an unprecedented velocity. The practical realization of quantum computer faces challenge such as decoherence, which need to be overcome to fully harness the powerless of principle of superposition. Despite these challenge, principle of superposition remains an excise and promising conception with wide-ranging deduction for the hereafter of computing and engineering.

ENTANGLEMENT

In the kingdom of quantum computer science, one of the most intriguing and fundamental phenomenon is entanglement. Web is the phenomenon in which two or more atom become interconnected in such a manner that the province of one atom cannot be described independently of the province of the other atom, regardless of the length between them. It is a unique characteristic of quantum mechanism that defies classical hunch and has far-reaching deduction for various fields, including artificial intelligence service and blockchain engineering. At its nucleus, entanglement originate from the principle of superposition rule, which allows quantum system to exist in multiple state simultaneously. When two or more atoms, such as photon or electron, are brought close together and interact with each other, their quantum state can become entangled. This web is not like any ordinary connection ; it is a mysterious and nonlocal core relativity that surpasses our classical apprehension of reason and consequence. Even when separated by vast distance, the entangled atom exhibit instantaneous correlation, as if they were still intimately connected. The conception of web was first introduced by Prince Albert Einstein, Boris Pools, and Nathan Rose in the famous EPR (Einstein-Podolsky-Rosen) paradox. They were troubled by the deduction of web, as it seemed to violate the rule of vicinity and challenged the thought of a deterministic existence. In their thought experimentation, they envisioned two entangled atoms being created and separated, with each atom observed by a different perceived. According to quantum mechanism, the measuring of one atom's province would instantaneously determine the province of the other atom, regardless of the length between them. This apparent misdemeanor of the velocity of visible light led Albert Einstein to famously describe web as "spooky activity at a length". Web has since been experimentally confirmed through various trial and has become an essential resourcefulness for quantum technology. One of the most impressive presentation of web occurred in 2012 when scientist at the university of Austrian capital successfully entangled two atoms separated by a length of 1.3 kilometer. By exploiting the phenomenon of web, research worker are now exploring the potentiality of quantum communicating network, which would enable secure transmittal of info over long distance without the fearfulness of listen in. Entanglement enable quantum teleportation, a procedure in which the province of an atom is transferred from one placement to another, without physically traversing the infinite in between. The deduction of entanglement widens beyond the kingdom of quantum computer science and communicating. The battlefield of artificial intelligence service is also beginning to harness web for novel computational technique. In classical computer, info is processed in binary word form, represented by spot that can be either 0 or In quantum computer, info is processed in qubits, which can exist in a principle of superposition of both 0 and 1 simultaneously. This principle of superposition allows for parallel calculation, enabling quantum computer to solve certain problem much faster than classical computer. Web plays a crucial function in quantum algorithm, such as Shor's algorithmic rule, which is able to factor large Numbers exponentially faster than classical algorithm. This algorithmic rule poses a significant menace to the protection of current encoding method, as it can break the widely used RSA encoding strategy. By leveraging the powerless of web, quantum computer could potentially revolutionize the battlefield of cryptanalysis and reshape the landscape painting of cybersecurity. Web has also found application in blockchain engineering, the underlying engineering behind cryptocurrencies like Bitcoin. Blockchain trust on cryptographic technique to ensure the protection and unity of minutes and maintain a distributed Leger that is resistant to tampering. With the coming of quantum computer, the current cryptographic method used in blockchain may become vulnerable to attack. By incorporating entanglement-based quantum cryptanalysis method, it may be possible to enhance the protection of blockchain system and protect against future quantum menace. In decision, web is a fascinating and fundamental phenomenon in quantum mechanism that defies classical hunch. It has incredible deduction for various fields, including artificial intelligence service and blockchain engineering. From enabling procure quantum communicating network to revolutionizing computational powerless in quantum computer, entanglement offers a glance into the untapped potentiality of quantum technology. As our apprehension of web intensify, we may uncover new possibility that will transform the manner we process info and interact with the surrounding universe.

QUANTUM BITS (QUBITS)

Quantum spot, or qubits, are a fundamental conception within the kingdom of quantum computer science and play a crucial function in harnessing the powerless of quantum info process. Unlike classical spot, which encode info in binary word form (either 0 or 1), qubits exist in a principle of superposition of state, allowing for a more extensive scope of possibility. This principle of superposition arises from the practical application of quantum mechanism principle, such as the rule of principle of superposition and the phenomenon of quantum web. In classical computer science, spot are the basic unit of measurement of info process, represented by electrical or physical state that can be 0 or These spot are processed through logic Gates, enabling the executing of algorithm and calculation. Quits differ significantly from classical spot because they take vantage of quantum phenomenon, which enable them to hold multiple state simultaneously. In quantum computing system, qubits can be realized using various physical system, such as trapped ion, superconducting circuit, or even encoded in the state of individual atom or photon. Regardless of the physical execution, the key facet of qubits lie in their power to exist in principle of superposition state, where they can be simultaneously 0 and These belonging allows quantum computer to process larger sum of info simultaneously, potentially providing exponential acceleration compared to classical computer science. The principle of superposition of qubits originate from the rule of principle of superposition, which states that a quantum scheme can be in a combining of multiple state at the same clip. This phenomenon is fundamentally different from classical mechanism, where a scheme is typically restricted to a single province. In the linguistic context of qubits, this means that a qubit can occupy state that correspond to both 0 and 1, but also any combining of these state. For illustration, a qubit can be in a province that is 70 % 0 and 30 % 1 simultaneously, representing a principle of superposition of these state. The powerless of quantum computer science is amplified through the conception of quantum web. Web occurs when two or more qubits become correlated in such a manner that the province of one qubit cannot be described independently of the others. This phenomenon allows qubits to be interconnected and enables the creative activity of quantum Gates, which are the quantum equivalent weight of classical logical system Gates. Quantum Gates, combined with principle of superposition and web, form the base for performing quantum calculation and algorithm. The potentiality of qubits in quantum computing lie in their power to manipulate and process large sum of info simultaneously. While classical computer process info sequentially, quantum computer can exploit the correspondence provided by principle of superposition. These belonging opens up new possibility for solving complex computational problem that are currently intractable for classical computer. Harnessing the powerless of qubits comes with numerous challenge. One major dispute lies in maintaining the coherency of qubits, as they are highly susceptible to environmental dissonance and intervention. Quits can lose their principle of superposition and entanglement state rapidly, which is referred to as decoherence. Overcoming decoherence is a critical facet of edifice practical and scalable quantum computing machine system.

Another dispute pertaining to qubits is the number of error rectification. Mistake can occur during calculation due to various factors, including environmental dissonance and fabrication imperfection. To ensure the dependability of quantum calculation, mistake rectification technique must be implemented to detect and correct mistake. Error rectification in quantum system is inherently complex due to the delicate nature of qubits and the no-cloning theorem, which states that it is impossible to create transcript of an unknown quantum province. In decision, qubits are a central constituent of quantum computer science, offering the potentiality for dramatically enhanced computational powerless. Through principle of superposition and web, qubits can store and process a vast sum of info simultaneously, providing the base for quantum algorithm and calculation. Challenge related to maintaining coherency and implementing mistake rectification technique remain significant hurdling in realizing practical quantum computing machine system. Nevertheless, the battlefield of quantum computing continues to advance, fueled by ongoing inquiry and technological promotion, bringing us one measure closer to unlocking the full potentiality of qubits and realizing the hope of quantum computer science.

CURRENT STATE OF QUANTUM COMPUTING

Quantum computer science has rapidly emerged as one of the most promising area of inquiry within the battlefield of engineering. This cutting-edge engineering holds the potential to revolutionize various sectors, from scientific inquiry to financial mold. Despite its immense potentiality, quantum computer science is still in its nascent phase, with many challenge and restriction that need to be overcome before it can become widespread. One of the key challenge in quantum computer science is the number of scalability. Traditional computer operate using spot, which can represent either a 0 or a In direct contrast, quantum computer use qubits, which can represent both 0 and 1 simultaneously due to a quantum belongings called principle of superposition. This allows quantum computer to perform massively parallel calculation, potentially leading to exponential acceleration in certain algorithm. Maintaining the delicate quantum province of qubits become increasingly difficult as the figure of qubits addition, due to the unavoidable fundamental interaction with the surrounding environs. This phenomenon, known as decoherence, makes it challenging to build quantum computer with a large figure of qubits, thus limiting their computational powerless. To day of the month, the largest quantum computer built have only a few tens of qubits, rendering them incapable of outperforming classical computer for most practical undertaking. There have been notable discovery in recent old age that have fueled optimism in the battlefield. For case, Google's quantum computing machine, called sycamore, achieved a major milepost in 2019 by performing a computation that would take a classical supercomputer a thousand of old age to complete. This so-called quantum domination experimentation marked a significant measure forward in demonstrating the potentiality of quantum computer. Another significant obstruction in the evolution of quantum computer science is the number of error rectification. Quantum system are extremely sensitive to mistake, and even small disturbance can cause the quantum province to prostration. To overcome this dispute, research worker are developing error-correcting code that can protect the quantum province against mistake. These code involve encoding the quantum info redundantly and using sophisticated mathematical technique to detect and correct mistake. While mistake rectification has been achieved in small-scale quantum system, scaling up these error-corrected system remains a formidable undertaking. The physical execution of qubits present a significant vault. Quits can be realized using an assortment of physical system, such as superconducting circuit, trapped ion, or topological state of affair. Each of these platform has its own advantage and restriction, and research worker are actively exploring different approach to improve qubit public presentation and scalability. For illustration, Microsoft is pursuing a topological qubit designing, which is less susceptible to decoherence and has the potentiality for long coherency multiplication. Building practical qubits that are stable, scalable, and highly coherent remains a major dispute. Despite the challenge, the battlefield of quantum computer science is advancing rapidly, with significant investing and involvement from both academe and manufacture. Major engineering company, such as IBM, google, and Microsoft, are investing heavily in quantum inquiry and evolution. Government around the universe are recognizing the potentiality of quantum computer science and are allocating significant resource to support its growing. For illustration, the United States recently passed the national quantum enterprise act, which aims to accelerate the evolution of quantum technology and establish a national quantum info scientific discipline inquiry plan. In decision, while quantum computer science is still in its early phase, it holds immense potentiality to revolutionize various fields. Despite the challenge of scalability, mistake rectification, and physical execution, significant advancement has been made in recent old age, demonstrating the powerless of quantum computer. As research worker and engineer continue to push the boundary of quantum engineering, it is anticipated that the current province of quantum computer science will continue to evolve, paving the manner for a hereafter where quantum computer can address complex problem that are infeasible for classical computer.

APPLICATIONS AND IMPACT OF QUANTUM COMPUTING

Application and wallop of quantum computing holds great potential to revolutionize various fields due to its power to solve complex problem at a significantly faster charge per unit than classical computer. One of the most promising application of quantum computing lie in the battlefield of cryptanalysis. Currently, encoding algorithm rely on the immense computational powerless required to crack them, which effectively deters potential attacker. With the coming of quantum computer, this algorithm can be easily broken, rendering current encoding method obsolete. Quantum cryptanalysis, on the other minus, offers a potential answer to this job by providing secure encoding using quantum key statistical distribution protocol. This protocol rely on the principle of quantum mechanism to establish procure communicating channel, ensuring that any listen in attempt are easily detected. By utilizing the property of quantum web and principle of superposition, quantum key statistical distribution can provide a degree of protection that is practically unbreakable, even for quantum computer. Another promising practical application of quantum computer science is in optimization problem. Many real-world problem, such as path optimization, programming, and provision concatenation direction, require finding an optimal answer among a vast figure of possible option. Classical computer struggle to efficiently solve this problem due to the exponential growing of calculation clip as the job sizing addition. Quantum computer, however, can leverage their inherent correspondence to explore multiple potential solution simultaneously, significantly speeding up the optimization procedure. This paleness can lead to significant improvement in numerous industry, such as logistics, transportation system, and finance, where finding the most efficient solution can greatly impact operational cost and overall public presentation. The battlefield of dose find and evolution can greatly benefit from the powerless of quantum computer science. Traditional method of dose find involve testing vast library of compound against specific target to identify potential campaigner for further evolution. This procedure is time-consuming, costly, and often output limited consequence. Quantum computing can assist in simulating and modeling molecular interaction at an unprecedented degree of truth and item. By utilizing quantum simulation, research worker can gain deeper penetration into how drug interact with target, significantly speeding up the procedure of identifying lead compound and predicting their pharmacological property. This computational powerless can accelerate the evolution of new drug, potentially leading to breakthroughs in treating disease that currently have limited intervention option, such as malignant neoplastic disease, Alzheimer's, and HIV/AIDS. Quantum computer science has the potential to revolutionize simple machine acquisition and artificial intelligence service algorithm. Quantum simple machine learning algorithm can leverage the powerless of quantum computer to process and analyze large datasets more efficiently. This paleness can lead to more accurate prediction, faster training multiplication, and improved form acknowledgment. One of the key advantage of quantum simple machine learning lie in its power to leverage principle of superposition and web to explore multiple potential solution simultaneously, allowing for faster convergence and better optimization of complex acquisition model. This can greatly enhance the capability of artificial intelligence service system, enabling them to solve more complex problem and make more accurate decision in real-time. In decision, quantum computer science has the potential to reshape numerous industry and fields. From revolutionizing cryptanalysis to accelerating optimization problem, dose find, and simple machine acquisition algorithm, the wallop of quantum computer science is far-reaching. While quantum computer are still in their nascent phase, ongoing inquiry and evolution attempt are rapidly advancing the battlefield. As quantum computing continues to mature and become more accessible, we can expect to witness even greater promotion and application in the old age to come. It is important to address the challenge associated with quantum computing, such as mistake rectification, scalability, and the ethical deduction of its immense computational powerless. By overcoming these challenge, we can harness the full potentiality of quantum computer science and unlock a new epoch of technological invention and scientific find.

CRYPTOGRAPHY

Cryptanalysis is a fundamental facet of procure communicating and info protective covering in the modern digital epoch. It involves method and technique used to convert plaintext info into unreadable information, also known as ciphertext, making it incomprehensible to unauthorized entity. Cryptanalytic algorithm and protocol play a significant function in ensuring the confidentiality, unity, and genuineness of digital information. The battlefield of cryptanalysis has witnessed significant promotion over the old age, driven by the increasing demand for secure minutes, sensitive information protective covering, and privateers saving. One of the most widely used cryptographic technique is symmetric key encoding. In this attack, the same secret tonality is used for both encoding and decoding of information. The tonality is shared between the transmitter and the intended receiver, providing a procured and efficient agency of communicating. This attack faces several restrictions, including the dispute of securely exchanging the tonality in the first topographic point. To address this, asymmetric tonality encoding, or public-key cryptanalysis, was introduced. Public-key cryptanalysis revolutionized the battlefield of cryptanalysis by introducing the conception of using different key for encoding and decoding. The encoding tonality, also known as the public tonality, is made available to everyone, while the corresponding decoding tonality, or private tonality, is kept securely by the key bearer. This proficiency solved the key statistical distribution job and opened up new possibility for secure communicating on a global scale of measurement. One of the most widely used asymmetric encoding algorithm is the RSA algorithmic rule, which is based on the trouble of factoring large prime Numbers. Another important facet of cryptanalysis is cryptographic hash function. This function are used to transform an input signal of any sizing into a fixed-size end product, or hash economic value. The main feature of hash function is that they are one-way and deterministic, meaning that given a hashish economic value, it is computationally infeasible to derive the original input signal. These belonging makes hash function ideal for information unity confirmation, as even a small alteration in the input signal information will result in a completely different hashish economic value. Cryptographic hashish function are used for watchword storehouse, digital signature, and various other protection application. With the rapid promotion in engineering, cryptanalysis is facing new challenge and opportunity. The ascent of AI has opened up new possibility for both attacker and defender. While AI can be used to enhance the capability of cryptographic algorithm and protocol, it can also be exploited to break them. AI algorithm, such as simple machine acquisition, can be trained to analyze large sum of encrypted information and place form, potentially exposing vulnerability in cryptographic system. On the other minus, AI can also be used to improve the efficiency and protection of cryptographic algorithm, such as by enhancing key coevals technique or optimizing encoding and decoding procedure. The outgrowth of new technology, such as Blockchain and quantum computer science, poses both menace and opportunity for the battlefield of cryptanalysis. Blockchain, a distributed Leger engineering, trust heavily on cryptographic technique to

170

ensure the immutableness and protection of minutes. Crypto-graphic hashish function are used in Blockchain to link block to-gether, creating an unalterable concatenation of record. Public-key cryptanalysis is used to secure minutes and establish reli-ance among participant in a decentralized web. New crypto-graphic algorithm and protocol must be developed to address the specific challenge brought by Blockchain, such as the de-mand for efficient consensus algorithm and privacy-preserving technique. Quantum computer science, on the other minus, has the potential to render many of the existing classical crypto-graphic algorithm disused. Unlike classical computer, which use spot to represent and process info, quantum computer utilize quantum spot, or qubits, which can exist in multiple state sim-ultaneously. This enables quantum computer to perform certain calculation exponentially faster than classical computer. As a consequence, algorithm that are currently considered procure, such as RSA and elliptic curve cryptanalysis (error correction code), can be easily broken by a powerful quantum computing machine. The evolution of quantum-safe cryptographic algo-rithm, often referred to as post-quantum cryptanalysis, is of overriding grandness to ensure the long-term protection of dig-ital information. In decision, cryptanalysis is a crucial battlefield that plays a vital function in ensuring the protection and unity of digital information. From symmetric and asymmetric encod-ing algorithm to cryptographic hash function, cryptanalysis pro-vides a base for procure communicating, secure minutes, and information privateers. With the promotion in AI, Blockchain, and quantum computer science, new challenge and opportunity arise, requiring continuous invention and evolution in the battle-field of cryptanalysis. As engineering continues to evolve, so must our cryptographic technique to adapt to the ever-changing landscape painting of digital protection.

OPTIMIZATION PROBLEMS

Another significant practical application of AI is in solving optimization problem. Optimization problem involve finding the best answer or combining of variable that maximize or minimize a certain objective mathematical function. This problem is prevalent in various area, such as technology, finance, logistics, and fabrication, where organization seek to optimize their procedure, resource, or end product. AI technique, particularly simple machine learning algorithm, have shown great hope in solving optimization problem. This algorithm can analyze large datasets and identify form and relationship that are not easily discernible through traditional method. By leveraging these form, simple machine learning algorithm can identify optimal solution or estimate to optimization problem. One illustration of an optimization job that AI can address is the traveling salesman job (TSP) . This job involves finding the shortest possible path for a salesman to visit a serial of city and tax return to the origin metropolis, while visiting each metropolis only once. The TSP is NP-hard, significance that it is computationally challenging to find the optimal answer as the figure of city addition. AI algorithms, such as genetic algorithm and simulated tempering, can provide near-optimal solution by iteratively improving upon initial solution through a procedure of mutant and choice. Similarly, AI can be applied to resource allotment problem, where organization need to allocate their resource, such as labor, stock list, or facility, in the most efficient and effective manner. For illustration, in fabrication, AI algorithm can optimize product agenda to minimize cost, reduce idle clip, and improve resourcefulness use. This algorithm can consider various constraint, such as simple machine capability, work force handiness, and client requirement, to develop optimal product plan that maximize productiveness while meeting client requirement. AI can be used to optimize financial portfolio. Portfolio optimization aims to allocate asset in a manner that maximizes tax return while minimizing hazard. Traditionally, this is done by diversifying investing across different plus class, such as stock, chemical bond, and commodity. AI technique can go beyond traditional variegation scheme by analyzing historical information, marketplace tendency, and other relevant factor to identify optimal plus allotment. Machine learning algorithm can learn from past marketplace behavior and apply this cognition to predict future marketplace motion, thus providing more robust and accurate recommendation for portfolio optimization. AI can be employed in logistics and provision concatenation direction to optimize the motion and statistical distribution of good and material. This involves determining the most efficient path for transportation system, optimizing storage warehouse configuration, and coordinating stock list degree. AI algorithm can consider various factors, such as transportation system cost, bringing multiplication, and client location, to develop optimal logistics plan that minimize cost and lead multiplication while maximizing client gratification. Apart from traditional optimization problem, AI can also be used to solve combinatorial optimization problem, where the answer infinite is extremely large and complex. Combinatorial optimization problem involve selecting the best combining or agreement from a finite exercise set of possibility. For case,

174

AI algorithm can be applied to the occupation store scheduling job, where machine and occupation need to be scheduled in the most efficient mode to minimize overall product clip. By leveraging genetic algorithm or other heuristic method, AI can identify near-optimal solution to these complex programming problem. In decision, optimization problem are prevalent in various spheres, and AI technique, particularly simple machine learning algorithm, offer effective solution to this problem. By analyzing large datasets, identifying form, and applying optimization technique, AI algorithm can provide near-optimal solution or estimate to complex and computationally challenging optimization problem. Whether it be in solving TSP, resourcefulness allotment, portfolio optimization, logistics preparation, or combinatorial optimization problem, AI has the potential to revolutionize these fields and enable organization to achieve higher efficiency, productiveness, and profitableness. With ongoing promotion in AI engineering, the capability to solve optimization problem will only continue to grow, resulting in numerous benefit for club as a unit.

DRUG DISCOVERY

Drug find is a complex and time-consuming procedure that involves the designation and evolution of new medicine or therapeutic agent. It plays a crucial function in improving human wellness and wellbeing by addressing various disease and medical weather. Traditional method of dose find are often associated with high cost, long timeline, and low achiever rate. In recent old age, AI, blockchain, and quantum computing have emerged as innovative technology that have the potential to revolutionize the battlefield of dose find. AI has increasingly been used in dose find to accelerate the procedure of identifying and developing new drug. Machine learning algorithm, for illustration, have been utilized to analyze large volume of information and identify novel dose campaigner with higher preciseness and truth than traditional method. AI is particularly useful in the initial phase of dose find, where it can efficiently sift through vast database of chemical substance compound and predict their potential therapeutic personal effects. AI can also aid in the optimization and alteration of existing dose campaigner, leading to improved officiousness and reduced face personal effects. Blockchain engineering has also shown tremendous potentiality in dose find by enhancing information protection, transparency, and coaction. Drug find involves the aggregation and analytic thinking of vast sum of sensitive affected role information, which must be protected to ensure patient privateers and confidentiality. Blockchain engineering offers a decentralized and secure political platform for sharing and storing

177

such information. It utilizes cryptographic technique and distributed ledger to ensure the unity and immutableness of information, thereby reducing the hazard of information use or unauthorized entrée. Blockchain enable improved coaction between different stakeholder in the dose find procedure, such as pharmaceutical company, academic institution, and regulatory government. It allows for the unlined and secure interchange of info, simplifying the communion of inquiry determination, clinical test consequence, and regulatory certification. Quantum computer science, although still in its nascent phase, holds significant hope for dose find. Traditional computer use spot, which are binary unit of measurement of info represented by either 0 or Quantum computer, on the other minus, utilize quantum spot, or qubits, which can exist simultaneously in multiple state. These belongings of qubits let quantum computer to process info in analogue, potentially enabling them to perform complex calculation and simulation at an exponentially faster charge per unit than classical computer. In does find, quantum computing can be utilized to model and simulate molecular interaction, protein folding, and drug-target interaction. By accurately predicting the behavior and property of chemical substance compound at a quantum degree, quantum computer can aid in the designing and evolution of new drug with enhanced officiousness and reduced perniciousness. Despite the tremendous potentiality offered by AI, blockchain, and quantum computer science, this technology also present certain challenge and restriction in the battlefield of dose find. AI, for illustration, heavily relies on the handiness of high-quality and well-curated information. In does find, obtaining such information can be challenging due to the deficiency of standardized and comprehensive database. AI

178

model may also suffer from bias and restriction stemming from the preparation information used. Careful circumstance should be given to the caliber and diverseness of the input signal information to ensure the truth and dependability of AI-driven dose find. Similarly, blockchain engineering faces certain challenge in the linguistic context of dose find. The acceptance of blockchain in the pharmaceutical manufacture requires the constitution of regulatory model and standard to address issue related to information privateers, accept, and possession. The scalability of blockchain network and the free energy ingestion associated with excavation trading operations need to be addressed to ensure the efficiency and sustainability of the engineering. Quantum computer science is still in its babyhood, and practical quantum computer capable of solving complex dose find problem are yet to be developed. Overcoming technical challenge, such as qubit staleness, mistake rectification, and scalability, is critical to the realization of the full potentiality of quantum computing in dose find. The integrating of quantum computing with existing algorithm and computational model used in dose find presents its own exercise set of challenge. In decision, AI, blockchain, and quantum computing have emerged as innovative technology with the potential to revolutionize dose find. This technology offer new approach for accelerating the designation and evolution of new drug, enhancing information protection and coaction, and enabling more accurate mold and computer simulation technique. They also pose challenge and restriction that need to be addressed for their effective integrating into the dose find procedure. It is crucial for research worker, pharmaceutical company, and regulatory body to collaborate and further explore the vast potentiality of this technology to improve

179

human wellness and wellbeing. AI, blockchain, and quantum computer science are three groundbreaking technology that have the potential to revolutionize various industry and sector. In recent old age, this technology have gained significant attending and are being explored for their power to bring unprecedented promotion in fields like health care, finance, and transportation system. AI is the subdivision of computing machine scientific discipline that aims to create intelligent machine that can mimic human behavior and perform undertaking that typically require human intelligence service. It encompasses fields like simple machine acquisition, natural linguistic communication process, and computing machine sight, making it a truly multidisciplinary battlefield. The outgrowth of AI has paved the manner for promotion in various sectors such as autonomous vehicle, virtual assistant, and health care topology. Blockchain, on the other minus, is a decentralized and transparent Leger scheme that record minutes across multiple computer. It gained widespread acknowledgment with the coming of cryptocurrencies like Bitcoin, but its application extends far beyond that. Blockchain can provide procure and transparent minutes, making it applicable in industry like finance, provision concatenation direction, and health care. Quantum computer science is a battlefield of computing that exploits the principle of quantum mechanism to perform calculation. Unlike classical computer that rely on spot to store and process info, quantum computer use quantum spot, or qubits, which exhibit principle of superposition and web property. Quantum computer science has the potential to solve complex problem that are currently intractable for classical computer, such as optimization and cryptanalysis. With this three technology rapidly evolving, their convergence has the potential to unlock unprecedented possibility. One country where the convergence of AI, blockchain, and quantum computing holds immense hope is healthcare. AI can be leveraged to analyze massive sum of medical information, enabling faster and more accurate diagnosis. By training simple machine learning model on vast sum of affected role information, AI algorithm can identify form and make prediction, assisting health care professional in identifying disease at an early phase. Blockchain can provide a decentralized and secure scheme for storing this sensitive medical information, allowing patient to have more control condition over their wellness record while maintaining privateers. The immutableness of blockchain can prevent meddling and ensure the genuineness of medical record, enhancing reliance between health care supplier and patient. When quantum computer science is introduced to this equality, it can further enhance AI's capability by processing complex calculation at an unprecedented velocity. Quantum algorithm can be used to analyze large datasets more efficiently, leading to improved diagnosing and intervention plan. Another country where the convergence of this technology has immense potentiality is finance. AI-powered chatbots and virtual assistant are already transforming client religious service in the financial sphere. These AI system can provide personalized recommendation, aid in financial preparation, and perform hazard appraisal. Blockchain can revolutionize the financial manufacture by providing procure and transparent minutes. Through the usage of smart contract, financial agreement can be executed automatically, eliminating the demand for mediator and reducing cost. In add-on, blockchain can facilitate cross-border payment by eliminating the demand for multiple mediator, making it faster and more cost-effective. Quantum computer science, in this linguistic context, can provide enhanced protection for financial minutes. Its power to perform complex calculation can be used to improve cryptanalytic technique, making financial minutes more procure and immune to chop. Transportation system is another sphere that stands to benefit greatly from the convergence of AI, blockchain, and quantum computer science. AI-powered autonomous vehicle can revolutionize transportation system, making them safer and more efficient. This vehicle can leverage AI algorithm to analyze real-time dealings information, optimize path, and improve rider refuge. Blockchain can enable procure and transparent ride-sharing service, allowing for efficient and trustworthy minutes between passenger and driver. The debut of quantum computer science can further enhance the capability of AI in transportation system. Complex optimization problem, such as dealings flowing direction and path preparation, can be solved more efficiently with the aid of quantum algorithm. As AI, blockchain, and quantum computing go on to evolve, their convergence holds immense hope in various sectors. From health care to finance and transportation system, this technology have the potentiality to transform industry, bringing unprecedented promotion and efficiency. Challenge such as ethical consideration, regulatory model, and substructure restriction need to be addressed for the successful integrating of this technology. Nonetheless, the possibility that lie ahead are vast, and the convergence of AI, blockchain, and quantum computer science is poised to reshape our universe as we know it.

V. INTERSECTION OF AI, BLOCKCHAIN, AND QUANTUM COMPUTING

The intersection point of AI, blockchain, and quantum computing represents a new frontier of engineering that has the potential to revolutionize the manner we live, piece of work, and behavior concern. AI is a subdivision of computing machine scientific discipline that focuses on the evolution of intelligent machine capable of performing undertaking that typically require human intelligence service. It encompasses various area, including simple machine acquisition, natural linguistic communication process, robotics, and computing machine sight. Blockchain, on the other minus, is a distributed Leger engineering that allows multiple party to maintain a shared database without the demand for a central authorization. It provides transparency, protection, and immutableness, making it ideal for application such as financial minutes, provision concatenation direction, and personal identity confirmation. Quantum computer science is a battlefield of survey that aims to utilize the principle of quantum mechanism to create powerful computer capable of solving complex problem at speed exponentially faster than classical computer. It takes vantage of quantum phenomenon, such as principle of superposition and web, to perform calculation that are beyond the range of classical computer science. The intersection point of these three technology presents exciting possibility and challenge. AI can benefit greatly from both blockchain and quantum computer science. Blockchain can enhance the transparency, protection, and unity of AI system by providing a decentralized and immutable phonograph record of information and algorithm. It can also enable procure and trusted collaboration between AI system and stakeholder, ensuring that the unity of AI-produced end product is upheld. The decentralized nature of blockchain can also address privateers concern by giving person control condition over their personal information and allowing them to selectively portion it with AI system. Blockchain can facilitate the incentivization of AI evolution and sharing through the usage of cryptocurrencies and smart contract. Quantum computer science, on the other minus, can exponentially accelerate AI calculation and enable the geographic expedition of new AI algorithm and model. The high-dimensional process powerless of quantum computer can solve optimization problem, imitate complex system, and improve simple machine learning algorithm, leading to more advanced AI capability. Quantum simple machine acquisition, for illustration, can exploit quantum algorithms to efficiently train model on large datasets and perform pattern acknowledgment undertaking with higher truth. It can also enhance the capability of AI in sphere such as dose find, logistics optimization, and financial mold. The integrating of AI, blockchain, and quantum computing can also bring about impactful application across various industry. In health care, for illustration, AI-powered system can analyze vast sum of medical information, including genetic info, affected role record, and clinical test, to diagnose disease, foretell result, and reinforcement personalized treatment. Blockchain can securely store and manage this sensitive wellness information, ensuring privateers and information unity. Quantum computing can further enhance AI's capability in analyzing biological system and designing novel drug. In finance, AI can be used to automate trade, detect imposter, and optimize investing scheme. Blockchain can provide a crystalline and tamper-proof phonograph record of financial minutes, reducing counterparty hazard and enabling faster colony. Quantum computer science can improve hazard appraisal model, develop more accurate price model, and optimize investing portfolio. The intersection point of this technology can also revolutionize provision concatenation direction by enhancing traceability, efficiency, and reliance. AI can leverage information from IoT device, satellite imagination, and other beginning to optimize stock list direction, improve logistics, and mitigate hazard. Blockchain can provide a procured and tamper-proof phonograph record of merchandise birthplace, ensuring that good are ethically sourced and authentic. Quantum computing can further optimize provision concatenation trading operations by solving complex optimization problem and simulating different scenario. Despite the potential benefit, the integrating of AI, blockchain, and quantum computer science also presents challenge. One of the key challenge is the scalability of this technology. For illustration, AI model require extensive computational powerless and large sum of information, which can be resource-intensive. Quantum computer, on the other minus, are still in their early phase of evolution, with limited qubits and fragile quantum state. Another dispute is the protection and privateers of this system. While blockchain provides protection feature such as encoding and consensus mechanism, it is not immune to hack and other attack. Quantum computer, with their huge process powerless, can also potentially break the cryptanalysis used to secure blockchain network. New cryptographic technique that are resistant to quantum attack need to be developed. In decision, the intersection point of AI, blockchain, and quantum computing represents a powerful convergence of technology that can transform various industry and society. The integrating of AI, blockchain, and quantum computing can enhance the transparency, protection, and efficiency of AI system, as well as exponentially accelerate AI calculation and enable the geographic expedition of new algorithm and model. This convergence also presents challenge, including scalability, protection, and privateers. Addressing these challenge will require coaction between research worker, engineer, policymakers, and stakeholder to ensure the responsible and ethical integrating of this technology.

IMPORTANCE OF THEIR CONVERGENCE

The convergence of AI, blockchain, and quantum computing holds immense import in various sectors of the economic system and club as a unit. This three technology, when combined, have the potential to revolutionize industry, heighten protection, and unlock unprecedented computational powerless. The interplay between AI, blockchain, and quantum computing enables the creative activity of highly intelligent system, secures the flowing of info, and facilitates complex calculation. One of the primary reason for the grandness of the convergence of this technology is their potential to revolutionize industry. AI, blockchain, and quantum computing individually have already shown their transformative powerless in various sectors, but their integrating has the potential to be truly revolutionary. For illustration, in the health care sphere, AI can be employed to analyze vast sum of affected role information and aid in topology and intervention decision. When combined with blockchain engineering, this information can be securely stored, shared, and accessed by relevant stakeholder. Quantum computing can facilitate complex simulation and calculation, enabling the designation of novel treatment and improving the overall efficiency of the health care scheme. Similar transformation can be seen in sector such as finance, transportation system, and logistics, where the convergence of this technology can lead to enhanced decision-making procedure, increased efficiency, and improved protection. The convergence of AI, blockchain, and quantum computer science also plays a crucial function in enhancing protection. One of the key challenges faced by organization and person nowadays is the growing menace of cyberattack and information breach. By combining AI, blockchain, and quantum computer science, it is possible to create highly secure system. AI can be utilized to detect and respond to cyber menace in real-time, identifying form and anomaly that human analyst may miss. Blockchain engineering, with its decentralized and immutable nature, provides a procure political platform for storing and sharing sensitive info, reducing the hazard of unauthorized entrée or meddling. Quantum computer science, on the other minus, can strengthen encoding algorithm, making it nearly impossible for hacker to break into secure system. The convergence of this technology holds the potential to address the pressing number of cybersecurity and safeguard critical info across various spheres. The convergence of AI, blockchain, and quantum computing enables the creative activity of highly intelligent system. AI, driven by simple machine acquisition algorithm, can analyze large datasets and learn from form, allowing for more accurate prediction and decision-making. When combined with blockchain engineering, this intelligent system can be used to automate minutes, establish digital identity, and facilitate smart contract. For case, AI-powered chatbots can provide personalized client religious service and reinforcement, while blockchain engineering can store dealing record securely, reducing the demand for mediator. Quantum computing can significantly enhance the computational powerless of AI system, enabling them to process and analyze information at an unprecedented velocity. The integrating of these technology opens up new possibility for developing intelligent system that can transform industry and improve citizenry's life. The convergence of AI, blockchain, and quantum computing facilitate complex calculation. Quantum computer science, with its power to perform parallel calculation, holds the potential to solve complex optimization problem that are currently intractable with traditional computer. By leveraging AI algorithm and technique, this quantum computer can be used to solve real-world problem more efficiently and effectively. For illustration, in the battlefield of logistics and provision concatenation direction, the integrating of AI, blockchain, and quantum computing can optimize path preparation, stock list direction, and bringing agenda, leading to cost nest egg and improved efficiency. In the battlefield of finance, complex hazard appraisal and portfolio optimization can be performed using the computational powerless of quantum computer, allowing for more accurate prediction and better-informed investing decision. The convergence of this technology unlocks the computational powerless necessary to tackle complex problem that were previously computationally infeasible. In decision, the convergence of artificial intelligence service, blockchain, and quantum computing holds immense grandness due to its potential to revolutionize industry, heighten protection, create highly intelligent system, and ease complex calculation. This technology, when combined, have the potential to address pressing societal and economic challenge and unlock unprecedented possibility. The integrating of AI, blockchain, and quantum computing enables the evolution of intelligent system that can transform sector such as health care, finance, transportation system, and logistics. It enhances protection by combining AI's real-time menace sensing capability with blockchain's procure and decentralized nature, further strengthened by the computational powerless of quantum computer science. The convergence of this technology paves the manner for a hereafter where business, government, and person can leverage their capability to drive invention, addition efficiency, and ensure the protection of critical info.

POTENTIAL SYNERGIES

Potential synergy between AI, blockchain, and quantum computing can revolutionize industry and significantly enhance technological capability. This three technology, although distinct, possess complementary property that can be leveraged to create a powerful confederation. AI brings advanced form acknowledgment, information analytic thinking, and decision-making capability to the tabular array. Blockchain, on the other minus, ensures transparency, immutableness, and protection in information minutes. Quantum computer science, with its power to process vast sum of information simultaneously, offer unprecedented computational powerless. When this technology converge, they create a political platform where AI algorithm can be deployed securely and efficiently, unlocking the full potentiality of AI application and providing cutting-edge solution to complex problem. The merger of AI and blockchain can also address the challenge of reliance, genuineness, and privateers, with the blockchain providing a decentralized model for securely storing AI-generated information. Quantum computing can vastly improve the velocity and efficiency of AI algorithm, enabling faster and more accurate prediction, optimization, and simulation. One country that can benefit from the synergy of this technology is healthcare. The integrating of AI, blockchain, and quantum computing can revolutionize medical diagnosing and intervention. AI algorithm can analyze vast sum of affected role information, including medical account, genetic info, and lifestyle factor, to identify form and make accurate diagnosis. The combining of AI and blockchain can address privateers concern by securely storing and sharing patient information while maintaining confidentiality. Blockchain's immutableness ensures the unity of medical record and prevents unauthorized alteration. Quantum computing can enhance the capability of AI algorithm in medical inquiry, enabling the process of large-scale genomic information, simulating the behavior of complex biological system, and facilitating dose find. With the integrating of this technology, personalized medical specialty can become a world, allowing for targeted treatment based on individual genetic and physiological feature. The usage of blockchain can enable decentralized network for health care information interchange, improving interoperability and facilitating coaction among healthcare supplier. Another sphere that can benefit from this synergy is cybersecurity. AI can be leveraged to detect and mitigate cyber menace by analyzing massive sum of information and identifying anomalous form. Blockchain can provide a procured and decentralized model for storing cybersecurity information, preventing unauthorized entrée and ensuring the transparency and unity of cybersecurity trading operations. Quantum computer science can significantly enhance cryptanalysis, enabling the evolution of quantum-resistant algorithm and strengthening information encoding. The integrating of this technology can create a robust cybersecurity ecosystem that can better protect organization from cyber-attacks and safeguard sensitive info. AI-powered blockchain analytics can track and trace the beginning of cyber menace, enabling proactive defense mechanism and facilitating the ascription of attack. The financial sphere can benefit greatly from the synergy of AI, blockchain, and quantum computer science. AI algorithm can analyze vast sum of financial information, identify marketplace tendency, and predict investing opportunity. Blockchain can provide a crystalline and immutable Leger for financial minutes, eliminating the demand for mediator and reducing dealing cost. Quantum computing can enhance financial mold, enabling faster and more accurate hazard appraisal and portfolio optimization. The integrating of this technology can create a more efficient and secure financial scheme, where AI-powered robot-advisors can provide personalized investing recommendation, smart contract can automate financial minutes, and quantum computing can enable real-time hazard direction and imposter sensing. Blockchain can address the challenge of financial comprehension by providing decentralized financial service to the unbanked universe, facilitating cross-border minutes, and reducing the dependence on traditional bank system. In decision, the potential synergy between AI, blockchain, and quantum computing clasp immense hope for revolutionizing industry and transforming technological capability. This technology, when integrated, can unlock new possibility in health care, cybersecurity, finance, and various other spheres. The combining of AI's advanced analytics, blockchain's transparency and protection, and quantum computing's computational powerless can create a powerful confederation that can address complex challenge and provide innovative solution. As this technology continue to evolve and mature, collaborative attempt and interdisciplinary inquiry will be crucial in harnessing their full potentiality and driving meaningful alteration in various sectors of the economic system.

PRIVACY AND SECURITY

Privacy and protection have become increasingly crucial concern in nowadays's digital historic period, as engineering continues to advance at an unprecedented gait. With the ascent of AI, blockchain, and quantum computer science, person and organization are faced with new challenge in protecting their sensitive information. AI, for case, has the potential to collect and analyze vast sum of personal info in slipway that were previously unimaginable. This raises concern about the potential abuse of this information and the potential encroachment of privateers. Similarly, blockchain engineering, which is designed to enhance protection and transparency, also poses certain hazard. While it offers procure and immutable record-keeping, it can also expose personal info through public ledger. Quantum computer science, with its unprecedented computational powerless, has the potential to break existing cryptographic algorithm, threatening the protection of information transmittal and storehouse. These issue highlight the demand for robust privateers and protection measure to ensure that person personal info remains protected. AI has emerged as a powerful instrument in various sectors, ranging from health care to finance, due to its power to procedure and analyze vast sum of information quickly. The aggregation and analytic thinking of personal info rise concern about the encroachment of privateers. AI system often requires entrée to personal information, such as person's medical record or online browse account, to provide accurate prediction and recommendation. While this information is often essential for the operation of AI algorithm, it also poses a hazard to person privateers. Misuse of personal information by malevolent party or even by the developer themselves can lead to serious consequence, such as personal identity larceny or unauthorized profile. It is essential to establish effective privateers model that regulate the aggregation, storehouse, and process of personal information in AI system. Blockchain engineering, on the other minus, was originally developed to enhance protection and transparency, particularly in the kingdom of digital currency such as Bitcoin. It also exposes personal info through public ledger, which are accessible to all user. Although these record are typically pseudonymous, it is still possible to trace minutes back to person, especially when combined with other available info. The immutable nature of blockchain airs challenge for person who want their personal info removed from the Leger. As blockchain becomes more widely adopted across various industry, including health care and provision concatenation direction, it becomes imperative to address this privateness concern and develop mechanism that allow person to control the vulnerability of their personal info. Quantum computer science is yet another engineering that brings both opportunity and hazard. Its unparalleled computational powerless has the potential to revolutionize many areas of scientific discipline and engineering. It also poses a significant menace to existing cryptographic algorithm. The fundamental principle that underpin modern encoding method, such as RSA or AES, rely on the trouble of factorizing large Numbers or solving complex mathematical equation. With the coming of quantum computer, this algorithm can be easily broken, leading to the via media of sensitive info. Consequently, it is crucial to develop quantum-resistant cryptographic algorithms that can withstand the computational capability of quantum computer. This would enable procure information transmittal and storehouse even in the front of quantum computer science. In decision, the rapid promotion of AI, blockchain, and quantum computing present exciting opportunity for club. It also brings forth privateers and protection concern that cannot be overlooked. The aggregation and analytic thinking of vast sum of personal information by AI system can invade person privateers if not adequately regulated. Similarly, blockchain engineering, although designed to enhance protection, exposes personal info through public ledger, posing hazard to person privateers. Quantum computing's immense computational powerless threatens the protection of information transmittal and storehouse by rendering existing cryptographic algorithm vulnerable. As this technology continue to evolve, it is essential to implement robust privateers and protection measure to protect person personal info and ensure a safe digital environs. By doing so, we can harness the full potentiality of this transformative technology while safeguarding individual right and personal information.

ENHANCED MACHINE LEARNING

Recently, there has been growing involvement in the battlefield of enhanced simple machine acquisition. Machine acquisition, a subset of artificial intelligence service, involves the evolution of algorithm and model that enable computer to learn from information and make prediction or decision without being explicitly programmed. Enhance simple machine learning takes this conception a measure further by incorporating advanced technique and technology to improve the truth and efficiency of simple machine learning algorithm. One such proficiency is deep acquisition, which uses artificial neural network to model and understand complex form and relationship in information. Deep acquisition has revolutionized various fields such as computing machine sight, natural linguistic communication process, and address acknowledgment, enabling machine to perform undertaking that were previously reserved for world. Another key engineering that enhances simple machine acquisition is the usage of big information. With the proliferation of digital device and the net, vast sum of information are generated every twenty-four hours. Big information provides simple machine learning algorithms with more divers and comprehensive datasets, which in bend enhance their power to make accurate prediction and decision. The coming of swarm computer science has greatly facilitated the process and analytic thinking of big information, making it more accessible and affordable for research worker and business alike. Cloud-based simple machine acquisition platform have emerged, allowing user to train and deploy simple machine learning model on a large scale of measurement with minimal substructure requirement. The combining of enhanced simple machine learning technique and big information process has paved the manner for discovery in various fields such as health care, finance, and transportation system. For illustration, in health care, enhanced simple machine learning algorithm have been developed to analyze medical image and detect abnormality with high truth. This has the potential to revolutionize diagnostic procedure and improve affected role result. In the financial sphere, simple machine learning algorithm combined with big information analytic thinking have been utilized to detect fraudulent activity and make more accurate prediction in inventory marketplace trade. This has not only reduced financial hazard but also increased investing tax return for person and institution. In transportation system, enhanced simple machine learning algorithm have been applied to optimize dealings flowing and improve the efficiency of transportation system. This has the potential to reduce over-crowding, lower emission, and improve overall transportation system experience for both person and business. While enhanced simple machine learning holds great hope, it also presents certain challenge and hazard that need to be addressed. One of the main challenge is the demand for large sum of high-quality labeled information to train simple machine learning model effectively. In many cases, acquiring such datasets can be time-consuming and expensive. The privateers and protection of big information pose significant concern. As more personal and sensitive information are collected for simple machine acquisition purpose, there is a greater hazard of information breach and unauthorized entrée. Regulation and ethical guideline must be put in topographic point to ensure the responsible usage and protective covering of information. The complexes and opaqueness of simple machine acquisition model pose challenge for interpretability and explain ability. Unlike traditional rule-based system, simple machine acquisition model operate based on statistical form and correlation that may not be easily understood by world. This deficiency of interpretability can limit the acceptance and reliance in simple machine learning system, especially in critical sphere such as health care and autonomous vehicle. Addressing this challenge and hazard requires a multi-faceted attack involving coaction between academe, manufacture, and authorities. Continued inquiry and evolution in enhanced simple machine acquisition technique are essential to push the boundary of what machine can learn and accomplish. Collaboration between information scientist, sphere expert, and policymakers is crucial to establish ethical guideline and regulation for information use and privateers protective covering. Attempt should be made to develop interpretable and explainable simple machine acquisition model, allowing user to understand and trust the decision made by this system. As simple machine learning become increasingly integrated into our daily life, it is important to ensure that it is used responsibly and ethically for the welfare of all. Enhance simple machine acquisition has the potential to revolutionize various fields and computer address complex problem that were previously considered unsolvable. By harnessing the powerless of advanced technique and technology, we can unlock the full potentiality of artificial intelligence service and progress club towards a new epoch of invention and find.

IMPROVED SCALABILITY

AI service, blockchain, and quantum computer science are undeniably revolutionizing the universe of engineering. In this paragraph, we will focus on the third subject, improved scalability, which refers to the power of this technology to handle larger and more complex datasets and calculation. One of the significant challenges faced by traditional computing system is their limited scalability. As datasets and calculation become increasingly larger and more complex, the power of conventional system to handle them efficiently diminishes. With promotion in artificial intelligence service, blockchain, and quantum computer science, improved scalability has become a world. AI service, or AI, plays a crucial function in achieving improved scalability. AI algorithm can analyze and process vast sum of information at an unprecedented velocity. With powerful simple machine learning technique, AI system can be trained to perform specific undertaking efficiently, thereby enhancing their scalability. For case, in the battlefield of mental image acknowledgment, AI algorithm can process a million of image within second, identifying form and object with remarkable truth. This improved scalability enables AI to handle complex undertaking that were once considered impractical or time-consuming, opening up new possibility in various spheres such as health care, finance, and transportation system. Blockchain engineering also contributes to improved scalability by revolutionizing the manner information is stored and processed. Traditional centralized database often faces challenge when scaling due to their single-point-of-failure nature. Blockchain employs a decentralized and distributed Leger scheme where information is stored across multiple node, ensuring enhanced scalability. Each city block in the blockchain contains a phonograph record of multiple minutes, forming an interconnected concatenation that is stored and validated by a web of computer. This decentralized construction enables blockchain to handle a larger bulk of minutes and calculation compared to traditional system. For illustration, cryptocurrencies such as Bitcoin and Ethereum can process a thousand of minutes per sec, making them suitable for scalable application. Quantum computing takes scalability to an entirely new degree by leveraging the principle of quantum mechanism. Traditional computer use spot, which can represent either a 0 or a Quantum computer use qubits, which can exist in a principle of superposition of both 0 and 1 simultaneously. This unique belongings of qubits let quantum computer to perform multiple calculation in analogue, exponentially increasing their process powerless and scalability. Quantum computer have the potential to solve complex problem that are virtually impossible for classical computer, including advanced optimization algorithm, molecular simulation, and cryptanalysis. The scalability offered by quantum computing opens up new avenue for scientific inquiry and technological promotion, promising discovery in fields such as dose find, financial mold, and clime scientific discipline. Improved scalability in artificial intelligence service, blockchain, and quantum computer science has far-reaching deduction. As this technology become more scalable, they enable novel application and promotion that were once considered inconceivable. For case, in the kingdom of artificial intelligence service, improved scalability allows for the evolution of more sophisticated and intelligent system. This has deduction across various industry, from autonomous vehicle that can navigate complex urban environment to personalized medical specialty that relies on AI algorithm to analyze vast sum of affected role information and provide tailored intervention plan. Improved scalability in blockchain engineering opens up new possibility for procure and transparent decentralized application that can handle large-scale information and minutes effortlessly. This has deduction for financial system, provision concatenation direction, and even voting system, where reliance and scalability are crucial. Improved scalability in quantum computing enable scientist to tackle complex problem and simulation that were previously beyond the capability of classical computer. This has the potential to revolutionize fields such as dose find, cryptanalysis, and clime mold, where scalability is key to achieving exact and meaningful consequence. In decision, improved scalability is a fundamental facet of the promotion in artificial intelligence service, blockchain, and quantum computer science. The power of this technology to handle larger and more complex datasets and calculation paves the manner for new application and discovery in various spheres. From AI system that can analyze and process vast sum of information to blockchain network that can handle large-scale minutes securely, and quantum computer that can solve problem exponentially faster than classical computer, improved scalability is revolutionizing the manner we approach engineering. As this technology continue to evolve, their scalability will play a crucial function in shaping the hereafter of invention, inquiry, and everyday living.

CHALLENGES AND CONSIDERATIONS

Challenge and consideration arsenic promise as the integrating of AI, blockchain, and quantum computer science may be, there are also significant challenge and consideration that must be addressed. One of the most significant challenges is the ethical deduction of using AI in various industry. With the immense powerless and capability of AI system, there is a growing care for issue such as privateers, prejudice, and occupation supplanting. AI system are designed to collect and analyze massive sum of information, which raises question about person privateers right. AI system have been known to perpetuate bias, as they learn from the information they are trained on. This can result in unfair decision-making procedure, particularly in area such as hire or loaning. The mechanization potentiality of AI poses a menace to occupation. As AI system become more advanced, there is a genuine care that they will replace human worker, leading to widespread unemployment and social agitation. Another dispute is the potential for cybersecurity hazard in blockchain engineering. While blockchain is touted for its protection feature, there have been case of breach and vulnerability in even the most secure system. Blockchain operates on a decentralized web, making it difficult for hacker to compromise the entire scheme. Individual node and wallet are still vulnerable to attack. There have been case of fraudulent initial mint offer (Icon) and Ponzi scheme in the blockchain infinite. These challenge highlight the demand for robust cybersecurity measure and regulatory inadvertence to ensure the unity and rustiness of blockchain system. Quantum computer science, although still in its nascent phase, also brings its own exercise set of challenge and consideration. One of the biggest challenges is the quest for stable quantum spot, or qubits. Quits are the fundamental unit of measurement of quantum computer science, and they are notoriously delicate and prostrate to mistake. Currently, research worker are experimenting with various physical system, such as superconducting circuit and trapped ion, to achieve stable qubits. This system face significant technical challenge, and it is uncertain when stable qubits will be widely available. Another circumstance is the wallop of quantum computing on encoding. Quantum computer have the potential to break many of the encoding algorithm used nowadays. This could have significant deduction for cybersecurity, as sensitive info that was once thought to be procured could be easily decrypted with quantum computer. As a consequence, there is a pressing demand to develop quantum-resistant encoding algorithm to protect information in the post-quantum epoch. The integrating of AI, blockchain, and quantum computer science requires significant computational powerless and resource. Quantum computer, in particular, are notoriously power-hungry and delicate, requiring specialized substructure and cooling system to maintain their staleness. As the requirement for AI, blockchain, and quantum computing turn, there is a demand to develop sustainable and efficient computing solution. This includes promotion in ironware, such as the evolution of more energy-efficient quantum processor, as well as software program optimization to maximize computational efficiency. The convergence of these technology raises legal and regulatory challenge. The rapid promotion in AI, blockchain, and quantum computing outpace the evolution

208

of regulation to govern their usage. This poses hazard in area such as information privateers, intellectual belongings right, and indebtedness. For illustration, the usage of AI algorithm and blockchain smart contract raises question about indebtedness in the case of autonomous scheme mistake or declaration dispute. The global nature of this technology necessitates international cooperation and harmonization of regulation to avoid legal conflict and facilitate cross-border collaboration. There are societal deduction to consider. The widespread acceptance of AI, blockchain, and quantum computer science will transform various industry and reshape the work force. While this technology offer significant benefit, such as increased efficiency and enhanced capability, there will also be break and supplanting. As occupation become automated, there is a demand to ensure that worker are equipped with the necessary skill and preparation to thrive in this new epoch. There is a demand to address the digital watershed and ensure equitable entrée to this technology, as the benefit should not be limited to a privileged few. In decision, the integrating of artificial intelligence service, blockchain, and quantum computing holds great hope for the hereafter. It is essential to address the challenge and consideration that come with this technology. Ethical concern, cybersecurity hazard, technical challenge, computational resource, legal and regulatory model, and societal deduction must all be carefully considered. By tackling these challenge, we can harness the full potentiality of AI, blockchain, and quantum computing to drive invention and create a better hereafter.

ETHICAL IMPLICATIONS

As we delve into the universe of AI, blockchain engineering, and quantum computer science, it becomes crucial to consider the ethical deduction that come along with this promotion. The rapid growing and integrating of AI system raises concern about privateers, liberty, and prejudice in decision-making procedure. With AI algorithms collecting and analyzing vast sum of personal information, there is a potential for breach of privateers and the abuse of sensitive info. The liberty of person may be compromised as AI system become more capable of making decision on their behalf. In case where AI algorithm are used for critical decision-making such as in autonomous vehicle or medical diagnosing, there are ethical consideration surrounding duty and answerability. Who should be held accountable for the decision made by AI system? How can we ensure that this decision are fair and unbiased? The transparency and explain ability of AI system are paramount to address this ethical concern and to build reliance between world and machine. Blockchain engineering, while offering potential benefit such as improved transparency and protection, also brings up ethical question. The decentralized nature of blockchain raise concern about the density of powerless and the potentiality for use. For case, if a choosey few hold the bulk of computing powerless in a blockchain web, they may influence decision and undermine the democratic ideal of equivalence and equity. The usage of blockchain in area such as provision concatenation direction and intellectual belongings right raises issue of privateers, as transactional information is stored indefinitely and accessible to all participant. The coming of quantum computing introduce a new exercise set of ethical deduction. While quantum computing promise immense computational powerless and the power to solve previously unsolvable problem, it also poses a menace to current encoding method. This has profound deduction for cybersecurity and privateers, as sensitive info could potentially be accessed and exploited by malicious actor. The ethical issue surrounding this technology require careful consideration and proactive measure to ensure that their deployment align with societal value and respect human right. A multidisciplinary attack that involves engineer, ethicist, policymakers, and the populace is essential to navigate the rapidly evolving landscape painting of AI, blockchain, and quantum computer science. By promoting transparency, answerability, and inclusivity, we can strive for the evolution of this technology in a responsible and ethical mode. In decision, as we embrace the transformative potentiality of artificial intelligence service, blockchain engineering, and quantum computer science, apprehension and addressing their ethical deduction becomes imperative. The ethical consideration surrounding privateers, liberty, prejudice, transparency, answerability, and the density of powerless require careful pilot age and proactive measure. With the multidisciplinary engagement of stakeholder, we can strive towards the evolution and deployment of this technology in a manner that upholds societal value and respect human right. As we shape the hereafter of AI, blockchain, and quantum computer science, let us ensure that our promotion are driven not only by scientific advancement but also by ethical consideration and a committees to the well-being of person and club as a unit.

REGULATORY FRAMEWORKS

Regulative model play a crucial function in effectively governing the rapidly evolving fields of AI, blockchain, and quantum computer science. With the continuous promotion and increasing acceptance of this technology, it becomes imperative to establish rule and regulation that safeguard the interest of various stakeholders. In the instance of AI, regulatory model must address ethical concern, information privateers and protection, indebtedness, and answerability. As AI system become more autonomous and capable of decision-making, question arise about their ethical behavior and potential bias. It is crucial for regulation to promote transparency and equity in AI algorithm and forestall favoritism against certain group or person. Information privateers and protection regulation are necessary to protect personal and sensitive info that AI system rely on. Ensuring that algorithm adheres to established privateers policy and securing information from cyber menace and breach are key challenge that regulatory model need to address. Similarly, in the instance of blockchain engineering, regulatory model are essential to capture its transformative potentiality while mitigating hazard. Blockchain, often associated with cryptocurrencies like Bitcoin, has the potential to revolutionize various sectors, including finance, provision concatenation direction, and health care. The decentralized and immutable nature of blockchain airs regulatory challenge. Establishing clear guideline for initial mint offer (Icon), cryptocurrency exchange, and smart contract is crucial to prevent fraudulent activity and ensure investor protective covering. Regulatory model must also address concern related to money wash, terrorist funding, and taxation equivocation that have been associated with cryptocurrencies. Striking a proportion between fostering invention and protecting stakeholder interest remains a key aim for blockchain regulation. Another country that requires thoughtful regulatory model is quantum computing. As quantum computer science progresses, it has the potential to disrupt current encoding method and posse significant deduction for national protection. Regulatory model must consider these concern and ensure that quantum computer science is harnessed responsibly and transparently. Developing encoding standard that are resistant to quantum attack should be a precedence. Regulatory model should address the ethical deduction of quantum computer science, particularly in the linguistic context of quantum simple machine acquisition and optimization algorithm. Clear guideline for the responsible usage of quantum computing in area such as finance, health care, and artificial intelligence service are crucial to mitigate potential hazard and ethical dilemma. Although regulatory model are essential, they must also be flexible and adaptable to cater to the rapidly changing landscape painting of this technology. Striking the right proportion between promoting invention and protecting societal interest is a complex undertaking that regulator face. Overly burdensome regulation could stifle invention and impede the potential benefit of this technology. Regulatory model should be designed in audience with manufacture expert, research worker, and other stakeholder to ensure they effectively address the unique challenge posed by AI, blockchain, and quantum computer science. International coaction and harmonization of regulation are also critical in this linguistic context. Given the global nature of this technology, inconsistent regulatory model across legal power can create challenge for business and hinder technological promotion. Establishing international standard and guideline can promote interoperability, foster cooperation, and allow for the seamless integrating of this technology across boundary line. Collaborative attempt through organization such as the International Organization for Standardization (ISO) and the international telecommunication union (ITU) can facilitate the evolution of harmonized regulatory model. In decision, regulatory model are of utmost grandness in governing the fields of artificial intelligence service, blockchain, and quantum computer science. This technology have the potential to revolutionize various industry and society, but they also pose unique challenge and hazard that necessitate clear guideline and regulation. Ethical concern, information privateers and protection, indebtedness, and answerability are some of the key area that need to be addressed in regulatory model. Striking a proportion between promoting invention and protecting stakeholder interest is essential. Flexibility, adaptability, international coaction, and harmonization of regulation are key factor that need to be considered to ensure effective administration of this transformative technology.

COMPUTATIONAL COMPLEXITY

Another prominent subject in the battlefield of artificial intelligence service and computing machine scientific discipline is computational complexes. Computational complexes mention to the survey of the resource required to solve a computational job. This resource can include clip, remembering, and communicating, among others. The survey of computational complexes aims to understand the inherent trouble of solving different type of problem and to develop efficient algorithms that can solve this problem within reasonable clip limit. There are various measure used to analyze the complexes of algorithm, and one of the most commonly used measures is clip complexes. Time complexes is concerned with the sum of clip required for an algorithmic rule to solve a job as a mathematical function of the input signal sizing. It provides an estimation of how long an algorithmic rule will take to run as the input signal sizing addition. This step is essential in understanding the scalability and efficiency of algorithm, especially when dealing with large datasets. One widely used notational system to describe the clip complexes of algorithm is Big oxygen notational system. Big oxygen notational system expresses the upper boundary of the growing charge per unit of an algorithmic rule's clip complexes. For illustration, an algorithmic rule with a clip complexes of oxygen (nitrogen) indicates that the algorithmic rule's running clip grows linearly with the input signal sizing. On the other minus, an algorithmic rule with a clip complexes of oxygen (1) has a constant run clip, regardless of the input signal sizing. Understanding the clip complexes of algorithm is crucial because it allows programmer and research worker to make informed decision about the scalability and efficiency of their codification. For case, if a particular algorithmic rule has a clip complexes of oxygen AI (n^2), it means that the algorithmic rule's running clip will grow quadratically as the input signal sizing addition. In such case, it might be necessary to consider alternative algorithm or optimize the existing codification to improve scalability. Aside from clip complexes, another important facet of computational complexes is infinite complexes. Space complexes is concerned with the sum of remembering required by an algorithmic rule as a mathematical function of the input signal sizing. Just like clip complexes, infinite complexes provides an estimation of how much remembering an algorithmic rule will consume as the input signal sizing addition. This step is particularly relevant in situation where remembering is limited, such as in embedded system or mobile device. Similar to clip complexes, infinite complexes can also be described using large oxygen notational system. For illustration, an algorithmic rule with an infinite complexes of oxygen AI (1) indicates that the sum of remembering required by the algorithmic rule remains constant, regardless of the input signal sizing. On the other minus, an algorithmic rule with an infinite complexes of oxygen AI (nitrogen) requires memory proportional to the input signal sizing. Being aware of infinite complexes is crucial in developing efficient algorithm, especially when dealing with large datasets. By understanding how an algorithm devour remembering, developer can optimize their codification and reduce remembering ingestion, leading to improved public presentation. Computational complexes also encompasses the survey of communicating complexes. Communication complexes focuses on understanding the sum of communicating required between different part of a distributed scheme. This step is particularly relevant in situation involving large-scale parallel process or distributed computer science. By analyzing the communicating complexes of a scheme, research worker can assess the efficiency and scalability of distributed algorithm, allowing for the designing of more efficient system. For illustration, in blockchain network, minimizing communicating complexes is crucial to ensure fast and secure minutes across the web. Computational complexes plays a significant function in various area of computing machine scientific discipline and artificial intelligence service. It allows research worker and practitioner to understand the intrinsic trouble of solving computational problem and to develop efficient algorithms that can tackle this problem within reasonable clip and resourcefulness constraint. By studying clip complexes, infinite complexes, and communicating complexes, expert in the battlefield can gain penetration into the restriction and capability of different algorithm, paving the manner for promotion in artificial intelligence service, blockchain, and quantum computer science. The evolution and promotion of artificial intelligence service, blockchain engineering, and quantum computer science are revolutionizing various sector and industry across the Earth. These three up-to-date technology are leading to significant transformation in different area such as finance, health care, transportation system, and even administration. As artificial intelligence service continues to evolve and improve, it is being integrated into a wide scope of application and system, enabling

219

machine to replicate human-like intelligence service and perform undertaking that were once exclusive to world. From chatbots and virtual personal assistant to autonomous vehicle and advanced robotics, AI is increasingly becoming an integral portion of our daily life. One of the key promotion in AI is simple machine acquisition, a procedure that allows machine to learn from information without explicitly being programmed. This power to learn and adapt makes AI machine highly efficient and capable of tackling complex undertaking. For case, in the battlefield of health care, AI-powered system are being used to diagnose disease, analyze medical image, and even develop intervention plan. This system are able to process vast sum of medical information and identify form and tendency that may go unnoticed by human doctor. Similarly, the outgrowth of blockchain engineering has brought about a prototype displacement in industry such as finance and provision concatenation direction. Blockchain is a distributed Leger that enables procure, crystalline, and decentralized minutes. It eliminates the demand for mediator and allows participant to establish reliance without relying on a central authorization. This engineering has significant deduction for financial minutes, as it provides a procured and tamper-proof phonograph record of all minutes, reducing imposter and enhancing answerability. Blockchain is also being used to enhance provision concatenation direction by providing transparency and traceability throughout the entire procedure. For illustration, the nutrient manufacture can use blockchain to track the beginning of merchandise, ensuring that they are sourced from ethical supplier and are safe for ingestion. Another engineering that is set to revolutionize the universe is quantum computing. Unlike classical computer that use spot to represent info, quantum computer use quantum spot or qubits, which can exist in multiple state at the same clip. These belongings of principle of superposition let quantum computer to perform complex calculation at an exponentially faster charge per unit compared to classical computer. In add-on to speed, quantum computer also have the power to solve problem that are currently considered unsolvable due to their complexes. Quantum computer science has the potential to unlock discovery in various fields such as dose find, optimization problem, and cryptanalysis. For case, pharmaceutical company can use quantum computer to simulate and understand the behavior of complex molecule, which will significantly speed up the dose find procedure. Similarly, optimization problem in industry like logistics and transportation system can be solved more efficiently using quantum algorithm, leading to cost decrease and improved efficiency. Despite their immense potentiality, this technology also bring about certain challenge and concern. With AI, there is an ongoing argument surrounding ethical motive and privateers. As AI system become more autonomous and capable of making decision, question arise about who is accountable in instance of mistake or injury caused by this system. There are concern about the privateers of personal information, as AI relies heavily on entrée to large sum of information to learn and function effectively. Similarly, blockchain engineering faces challenge related to scalability, free energy ingestion, and regulatory model. While blockchain provides transparency, protection, and decentralization, it also consumes a significant sum of free energy due to its consensus mechanism. Regulatory model around blockchain are still evolving, with government and policymakers grappling with the legal deduction and potential hazard associated with this engineering. Quantum computing present protection challenge, especially for current cryptographic system. The immense computational powerless of quantum computer could potentially break current cryptographic algorithm, compromising the protection of sensitive info. This has led to a subspecies to develop quantum-resistant cryptanalysis to ensure the protection of information in the quantum epoch. In decision, artificial intelligence service, blockchain engineering, and quantum computer science are driving major promotion and invention across various industry. AI is enabling machine to replicate human-like intelligence service, blockchain is revolutionizing industry by providing procure and transparent minutes, and quantum computer science is set to solve complex problem at an unprecedented velocity. Along with this promotion come challenge and concern regarding ethical motive, privateers, scalability, free energy ingestion, and protection. As this technology continue to evolve and mature, it is crucial to address these issue and ensure they are harnessed for the improvement of club.

VI. FUTURE IMPLICATIONS AND ETHICAL CONCERNS

The future deduction of the combining of artificial intelligence service, blockchain, and quantum computer science are vast and far-reaching. This technological promotion have the potentiality to transform industry and remold club in profound slipway. One of the most significant deductions is the potential for AI and blockchain to disrupt traditional industry and concern model. With AI's power to analyze large sum of information and make complex decision, business can streamline their trading operations, improve efficiency, and reduce cost. Blockchain, on the other minus, offer unprecedented transparency and protection, enabling business to create tamper-proof record and secure minutes. When combined, the powerless of AI and blockchain can revolutionize industry such as finance, health care, provision concatenation direction, and even authorities trading operations. In the finance sphere, AI and blockchain can enhance the efficiency and protection of minutes. For illustration, AI-powered trade algorithm can analyze marketplace information and put to death trade at lightning velocity, potentially reducing the hazard of human mistake and increasing profitableness. Meanwhile, blockchain engineering can provide an immutable Leger of minutes, enabling faster and more secure cross-border payment. AI can be applied to detect imposter and money wash activity, helping financial institution to comply with regulation and prevent economic crime. In health care, the integrating of AI and blockchain can lead to significant improvement in affected role attention and medical inquiry. AI algorithm can analyze massive sum of affected role information, identifying form and predicting disease early on. This can assist in delivering personalized treatment and improving patient result. Blockchain can enhance the protection and privateers of medical record through decentralized storehouse and encoding technique, ensuring that sensitive patient info remains confidential and tamper-proof. The use of this technology can also accelerate the dose find procedure, as AI algorithm can quickly analyze vast sum of scientific lit and identify potential dose campaigner, while blockchain ensures the unity and traceability of clinical test information. While this promotion bring about remarkable opportunity, they also raise ethical concern that need to be addressed. The first care revolves around occupation supplanting. As AI becomes increasingly capable of automating undertaking that were once exclusively performed by world, there is a concern about batch unemployment and economic inequality. It is crucial to ensure that the benefit of this technology are shared equitably, and that measure are put in topographic point to retrain and deskill worker whose occupation are at hazard of being automated. Another significant ethical care is the potential for prejudice and favoritism in AI algorithm. AI system are trained on large datasets that often reflect the bias present in club, leading to discriminatory result. For case, facial acknowledgment system have been found to display racial prejudice, misidentifying person with dark argument tone more frequently. To combat this, it is essential to develop and implement strict regulation that promote equity, transparency, and answerability in AI algorithm. Privacy is also an overriding ethical care in the historic period of AI, blockchain, and quantum computer science. The power of this technology to process vast sum of personal information raise concern about potential privateers breach and surveillance. It is crucial to establish robust information protective covering model that prioritize the privateers right of person, ensuring that information is handled securely and with accept. Blockchain's immutable nature raises question about the right to be forgotten and the permanency of info stored on the Leger. Striking a proportion between the benefit of transparency and the privateers right of person is a dispute that needs to be tackled. A final honorable care is the potential for autonomous AI system to act in slipway that are harmful or morally ambiguous. As AI algorithms become increasingly complex and autonomous, there is a hazard of unintended consequence or malicious usage. For illustration, in autonomous vehicle, the algorithm decision-making procedure can lead to ethical dilemma. Should a self-driving auto prioritize the refuge of its passenger over that of pedestrian ? The evolution of ethical guideline and regulation is necessary to ensure that AI system are designed and programmed with an exercise set of ethical principle and value. In decision, the combining of artificial intelligence service, blockchain, and quantum computing holds immense potentiality for transforming industry and society. From enabling more efficient financial minutes to enhancing health care result, this technology offer numerous benefit. Ethical consideration must not be overlooked. Addressing concern such as occupation supplanting, prejudice in algorithm, privateers breach, and the ethical behavior of autonomous system is paramount to ensure the responsible evolution and usage of this technology for the improvement of club. By adopting a proactive and multidisciplinary attack, we can harness the powerless of these technology while upholding ethical principle.

PREDICTIONS ON THE FUTURE INTEGRATION OF THESE TECHNOLOGIES

The integrating of artificial intelligence service, blockchain, and quantum computer science is widely expected to shape the hereafter of various industry and revolutionize the manner we live and piece of work. Expert predict that this technology will become increasingly intertwined, complementing and enhancing each other's capability. One major anticipation is the outgrowth of intelligent blockchain network that leverage the powerless of quantum computer science. As quantum computer become more powerful and efficient, they will be able to solve complex mathematical algorithm and cryptographic puzzle at an unprecedented velocity. This will greatly enhance the protection and scalability of blockchain network, making them more resilient to attack and capable of handling a vast figure of minutes. Quantum computing's power to analyze massive sum of information and place form will empower artificial intelligence service system to make more accurate prediction and informed decision. This integrating will enable smart contract to not only execute predefined weather but also adapt and evolve based on real-time information, leading to more dynamic and efficient concern procedure. The combining of this technology will enable real-time, tamper-proof audit and transparency in provision irons, financial system, and other industry. By utilizing artificial intelligence service algorithm to analyze blockchain information, company can gain valuable penetration into their trading operations, identify inefficiency, and streamline their procedure. The integrating of this technology is also expected to bring about significant promotion in health care. With artificial intelligence service's power to analyze large datasets, quantum computing's unparalleled computational powerless, and blockchain's immutable and transparent nature, the diagnosing and intervention of disease will be vastly improved. By leveraging the integrating of this technology, doctor and health care professional will be able to entrée and portion patient information securely, predict medical weather before they occur, and develop personalized intervention plan. The integrating of quantum computer science and blockchain will enhance the protection of medical record, protecting sensitive patient info from cyberattacks while still allowing authorized person to entrée it when needed. Another country where the integrating of this technology is predicted to have a profound wallop is the financial manufacture. AI service algorithm powered by quantum computer science will enable more sophisticated and accurate imposter sensing system. Machine learning algorithm will analyze massive sum of information in real-time, identifying suspicious activity and form that human analyst might miss. The transparency and immutableness of blockchain will further enhance the protection and unity of financial minutes, reducing the hazard of imposter and mistake. The integrating of this technology will democratize entrée to financial service. Blockchain-powered platform can provide procure and decentralized bank service to unbanked population, allowing them to store economic value, behavior minutes, and entrée loan without the demand for traditional financial mediator. The integrating of artificial intelligence service and blockchain could revolutionize the inventory marketplace. With simple machine learning algorithms analyzing vast sum of information, investor can make more informed decision, predict marketplace tendency, and identify profitable investing opportunity. The integrating of this technology will also have a significant wallop on the free energy manufacture. The combining of blockchain and renewable free energy beginning will enable the creative activity of decentralized free energy grid, where user can produce, consume, and craft free energy in a peer-to-peer mode. Blockchain-based free energy trade platform will allow person and business to buy and sell excess free energy directly, reducing dependence on centralized free energy supplier and promoting sustainability. By utilizing artificial intelligence service and quantum computer science, free energy company can optimize their trading operations, predict free energy requirement, and allocate resource more efficiently. This will result in a more sustainable and resilient free energy power system that can adapt to changing weather and handle the increasing requirement for clean free energy. In decision, the integrating of artificial intelligence service, blockchain, and quantum computer science is set to revolutionize various industry and reshape the hereafter. The intelligent integrating of this technology will lead to faster, more procure, and efficient system that can unlock unprecedented degree of invention and productiveness. From health care to finance, free energy, and beyond, the possibility for these integrated technology are vast and promising. As with any emerging engineering, there will be challenge and ethical consideration that need to be addressed. As we move forward, it is crucial to ensure that the integrating of this technology is guided by responsible and inclusive principle, bringing about positive alteration for club as a unit.

SOCIOECONOMIC IMPACTS

The outgrowth and promotion of artificial intelligence service, blockchain, and quantum computing have profound socioeconomic impact that are transforming various sectors across the Earth. In footing of AI, it's integrating into different industry, such as health care, finance, and transportation system, has revolutionized the manner piece of work is done, leading to increased productiveness and efficiency. AI-powered automaton and algorithm have the potential to take over repetitive and mundane undertaking, allowing human worker to focus on more complex and creative enterprise. This displacement in labor kinetics may result in occupation supplanting and break in the work force, as certain occupation become obsolete with the ascent of mechanization. It is essential to note that while AI may eliminate some occupation function, it also creates new employ opportunity in area such as information analytic thinking, simple machine acquisition, and AI evolution. The socio-economic impact of blockchain engineering are equally significant. Blockchain, a decentralized and transparent digital Leger, has the potential to transform various sectors, including finance, provision concatenation direction, and health care. The distributed nature of blockchain guarantee that all minutes are recorded and stored securely, reducing the hazard of imposter and use. In the financial sphere, blockchain has the potential to streamline procedure, eliminate mediator, and increase efficiency. Blockchain-based cryptocurrencies, such as Bitcoin, have emerged as alternative method of defrayal and investing, disrupting the traditional bank scheme. The widespread acceptance of blockchain engineering is not without its challenge. Issue related to scalability, privateers, and regulatory model need to be addressed to fully harness the potential socio-economic benefit of this groundbreaking engineering. Quantum computer science is another technological promotion with significant socio-economic impact. Unlike classical computer that store and process info in spot AI 0s and 1s), quantum computer use quantum spot or qubits, which can exist in multiple state simultaneously. This enables quantum computer to perform complex calculation at an unprecedented velocity, revolutionizing fields such as cryptanalysis, dose find, and optimization problem. Quantum computer science has the potential to break current encoding method, posing both opportunity and menace to cybersecurity. While it may enable more secure communicating protocol, it also presents challenge in footing of ensuring information privateers and protective covering. Quantum computer science has deduction for various industry, including finance, where it can enable faster and more accurate information analytic thinking and hazard appraisal. The widespread acceptance of quantum computer science is still in its early phase, with significant technological and substructure challenge yet to be overcome. The socio-economic impact of this transformative technology are not limited to specific sector but extend to society as a unit. The execution of AI, blockchain, and quantum computer science requires person and organization to adapt to rapidly changing technological landscape. This necessitates a continuous procedure of upskilling and deskilling to remain relevant in the occupation marketplace. The ethical deduction of this technology need to be carefully considered. For case, AI algorithm may perpetuate bias or consequence in prejudiced result if not properly developed, tested, and monitored. Similarly, the transparency and answerability of blockchain system need to be ensured to prevent abuse or use. The societal impact of mechanization and occupation supplanting demand to be addressed, with a focusing on providing reinforcement and opportunity for affected person to transition into new function or industry. The acceptance of this technology may exacerbate existing socio-economic inequality. As organization and person with greater entrée to resource and working capital put in AI, blockchain, and quantum computer science, there is a hazard of widening the digital watershed. It is crucial to bridge this watershed by promoting inclusivity and equitable entrée to this transformative technology. Government, policymakers, and educational institution play a vital function in ensuring that the benefit of this technology are distributed fairly, while also addressing the societal challenge that arise from their execution. In decision, the socio-economic impact of artificial intelligence service, blockchain, and quantum computer science are profound and wide-ranging. This technology have the potential to revolutionize industry, addition productiveness and efficiency, and create new employ opportunity. They also pose challenge such as occupation supplanting, ethical consideration, and socio-economic inequality. To fully harness the benefit of this transformative technology, a multi-faceted attack is required, with a focusing on continuous acquisition, ethical evolution, inclusivity, and equitable entrée. Consequently, the effective integrating of AI, blockchain, and quantum computing can shape a hereafter that is both technologically advanced and socially and economically inclusive.

ETHICAL CONSIDERATIONS

Ethical consideration In the historic period of rapid technological promotion, the ethical deduction of Artificial intelligence, blockchain, and quantum computing have become of utmost grandness. As this technology continue to develop and integrate into various sectors of club, the potential consequence they can have on person, community, and the overall ethical landscape painting cannot be ignored. One of the fundamental ethical consideration surrounding AI is the number of privateers and information protection. Given that AI relies heavily on vast sum of personal information to make accurate prediction and decision, there is a demand to ensure that this information is collected and used in an ethical mode. The unauthorized entrée or abuse of personal information can infringe upon a person's privateers right and Pb to severe consequence such as personal identity larceny or use. To address this care, ethical guideline and regulation must be put in topographic point to govern the aggregation, storehouse, and usage of information within AI system. Another ethical circumstance that arises from the promotion in AI is the potential wallop on employ and socioeconomic inequality. The mechanization and efficiency that AI provides can significantly disrupt industry and Pb to occupation supplanting. While this can bring about positive change in footing of productiveness and economic growing, it also raises concern about the potential deprivation of occupation and the widening spread between the rich and the poor. It is essential to ensure that the benefit of AI are distributed fairly and that adequate reinforcement and re-training plan are in topographic point to assist person who are at hazard of losing their support due to technological promotion. It is crucial to address any bias that may exist within AI algo-rithms that can perpetuate favoritism or unequal opportunity, as this can further exacerbate existing socioeconomic disparity. Blockchain, on the other minus, introduces a new exercise set of ethical consideration, particularly in the linguistic context of transparency and answerability. The decentralized nature of blockchain engineering offers potential solution for improving transparency and reliance, especially in area such as financial minutes and provision irons. It also raises concern about the po-tential abuse of this engineering for illicit activity and the trouble in holding person accountable for their action. Since the infor-mation stored on a blockchain is immutable and cannot be tam-pered with, there is a demand to ensure that the info recorded is accurate and verified. The evolution of smart contract and decentralized application should adhere to ethical principle to prevent fraudulent or malicious activity that can exploit vulner-ability within the scheme. Quantum computer science, an engi-neering that is still in its babyhood, present unique ethical chal-lenge. Its huge process powerless has the potential to revolu-tionize fields such as cryptanalysis and pharmaceutical inquiry. It also raises concern about the protection and privateers of sen-sitive info that could be compromised with the coming of pow-erful quantum computer. Encoding method currently used to safeguard sensitive information may become obsolete, posing a menace to person and organization alike. Ethical consideration surrounding quantum computing necessitate the evolution of ro-bust encoding method that can withstand the powerless of

236

quantum calculation, as well as the constitution of ethical guideline for the responsible usage of this engineering. In decision, the rapid advancement of AI, blockchain, and quantum computing call for careful circumstance of their ethical deduction. Ethical concern surrounding privateers and information protection, socioeconomic inequality, transparency, and answerability need to be addressed to ensure that this technology are developed and implemented in a mode that benefit club as a unit. The constitution of ethical guideline and regulation is crucial to govern the usage of personal information within AI system and prevent the unauthorized entrée or abuse of info. Measure should also be taken to mitigate the potential wallop of AI on employ and socioeconomic disparity, ensuring that the benefit of this technology are distributed equitably. Similarly, the evolution of blockchain and quantum computer science should adhere to ethical principle to promote transparency, truth, and the responsible usage of this technology. By addressing this ethical consideration proactively, club can harness the full potentiality of this technology while minimizing the potential hazard they pose.

DATA PRIVACY

Data privateers is a critical number in nowadays's digital club, where vast sum of personal info are constantly being collected and stored by various organization. With the rapid promotion in engineering such as AI, blockchain, and quantum computer science, the demand to protect person information privateers has become even more crucial. AI, for case, has the potential to greatly increase the efficiency and effectivity of information process and analytic thinking. It also poses significant challenge to information privateers as it collects and analyzes large volume of personal information. This raises concern about how this valuable info is being used and whether person privateers right are being adequately protected. Similarly, blockchain engineering, which promises procure and transparent minutes, also presents privateers concern. While blockchain ensures the immutableness and unity of information through its decentralized nature, it may limit privateers as all minutes are visible to all participant on the web. Concern arise as to how this transparency may impact privateers, particularly regarding sensitive info. Quantum computer science, with its transformative potentiality in information process and encoding, presents both opportunity and challenge for information privateers. On one minus, quantum computer science can enable stronger encoding method that protect personal info and procure information transmittal. On the other minus, it also introduces potential menace to existing encoding algorithm, making personal information more vulnerable to unauthorized entrée. This promotion in engineering rise important question about the proportion between invention, information privateers, and protection. In order of magnitude to address these concern, it is crucial to establish robust regulation and model that prioritize information privateers. Collaboration between government, organization, and person is essential to develop and implement effective scheme for protecting personal info. One key facet of information privateers is informed except. Person should have the right field to know how their information is being collected, stored, and used. Crystalline and easily understandable accept procedure should be in topographic point to ensure that person are fully aware of what they are agreeing to. Person should have the power to control their personal info, including the right field to request its omission or rectification if necessary. Another essential facet of information privateers is data minimization. Organization should only collect and retain the minimum sum of personal information necessary for a specific intent. The rule of information minimization helps reduce the hazard of unauthorized entrée and abuse of personal info. Information anonymization technique should be employed to protect person privateers even when information is being shared for inquiry or public wellness purpose. By removing personally identifiable info, anonymization can help mitigate the privateers hazard associated with information sharing. In add-on to regulation, technological solution can also play a crucial function in enhancing information privateers. For illustration, privacy-enhancing technology AI pet) such as differential privateers can be employed to protect person privateers while still enabling useful information analytic thinking. Derived function privateers adds dissonance to datasets to ensure that person personal info cannot be re-identified, thereby safeguarding their privateers. Similarly, encoding technique such as homomorphic encoding can allow person to maintain control condition over their information even when it is being used for calculation. Homomorphic encoding enable calculation to be performed on encrypted information without decrypting it, thus preserving the privateers of the underlying information. The execution of decentralized personal identity system can empower person to maintain control condition over their personal info. With decentralized personal identity, person can manage and portion their personal info in a procured and privacy-preserving mode. Using blockchain engineering, person can have greater control condition over their personal information, deciding who can entrée it and for what purpose. These decentralized personal identity system can provide a more user-centric and privacy-respecting attack to managing personal info. While promotion in engineering convey about concern for information privateers, they also offer opportunity to enhance privateers and protection. As AI, blockchain, and quantum computing go on to evolve, it is imperative that information privateers remains at the head of evolution. By implementing appropriate regulation, employing privacy-enhancing technology, and empowering person with control condition over their personal info, we can navigate the complexity of the digital historic period and ensure that information privateers is upheld while embracing the potential benefit of this technology. Only through a collaborative and multidisciplinary attack can we address the challenge and opportunity that arise in the linguistic context of information privateers.

BIAS AND FAIRNESS

Bias and equity are critical issue that need to be addressed when it comes to AI, blockchain, and quantum computer science. This technology have the potential to revolutionize various sectors, but they also raise concern about the prolongation of biased decision-making and unfair result. One of the main challenge with AI is the prejudice embedded in algorithm, which can result in discriminatory practice. AI system are trained on vast sum of information, and if this information is biased or lacks diverseness, the AI can inadvertently make biased decision. For illustration, facial acknowledgment system have been shown to have higher mistake rate when identifying citizenry of color or woman compared to white work force, highlighting the prejudice inherent in this technology. It is essential to ensure that the preparation information used for AI algorithm is representative and diverse to avoid perpetuate bias. Similarly, equity is a crucial circumstance when it comes to the usage of blockchain engineering. Blockchain, with its decentralized and transparent nature, has the potential to create fair and trusted system. The execution of blockchain in various spheres can also lead to unintended consequence. For case, in the battlefield of finance, the usage of blockchain for loaning or policy may inadvertently exclude certain person or group, leading to unfair result. The acceptance of blockchain engineering requires entrée to the net, which may further exacerbate existing inequality, as disadvantaged community might not have entrée to the necessary substructure. It is crucial to examine the potential deduction of implementing

243

blockchain and ensure that it does not perpetuate inequity or worsen existing inequality. Quantum computer science, although still in its early phase of evolution, also raises concern about prejudice and equity. Quantum computer have the potential to solve complex problem exponentially faster than classical computer, which could revolutionize industry such as dose find, cryptanalysis, and optimization. The algorithm used in quantum computer science may still be susceptible to biased or unfair result. Just as with classical computer, the preparation information used to develop quantum algorithm should be carefully examined to ensure fair and unbiased consequence. The entrée to and use of quantum computing resource should be equitable and crystalline to prevent the density of powerless or excommunication of certain group. Addressing prejudice and ensuring equity in the evolution and deployment of this technology requires a multi-faceted attack. Firstly, diverseness and comprehension should be prioritized when collecting and curating datasets for training AI algorithm. Ensuring that the information used is representative of diverse population will help prevent bias from being embedded in the AI system. Secondly, the evolution and deployment of AI, blockchain, and quantum computing should involve interdisciplinary collaboration and extensive ethical consideration. Ethical guideline and model should be developed and followed to ensure equity and mitigate prejudice. This guideline should be regularly updated to keep gait with the evolving engineering landscape painting. Auditability and explain ability are crucial for addressing prejudice and ensuring equity. Crystalline algorithm and system allow for examination and answerability, helping to identify and rectify bias. Blockchain's inherent transparency can contribute to this by allowing for the trace and confirmation of minutes. Attempt should be made to make AI algorithm interpretable, enabling user and stakeholder to understand the decision-making procedure and identify any potential bias. Education and public consciousness also play a significant function in promoting prejudice consciousness and equity. Educating person about the potential bias and ethical deduction of this technology can help foster a more informed and engaged club. It is essential to involve not only expert but also diverse stakeholder, including policymakers, concern leadership, and community of interests representative, in discussion surrounding prejudice and equity. This inclusive attack can help identify potential bias and ensure that decision about the usage of this technology are made collectively and ethically. In decision, addressing prejudice and ensuring equity in the evolution and deployment of AI, blockchain, and quantum computer science is a critical undertaking. Bias embedded in AI algorithm, unintended consequence of blockchain execution, and potential bias in quantum computing algorithms all rise concern about unfair result. To mitigate these issue, attempt should be made to ensure diverseness in preparation information, develop ethical guideline, promote transparency and explain ability, educate person, and involve divers stakeholder. By taking these stairs, we can harness the full potentiality of this technology while also ensuring equity and avoiding the prolongation of bias and inequality.

AUTONOMY AND HUMAN CONTROL

Another fundamental care regarding the execution of AI, blockchain engineering, and quantum computer science is the number of liberty and human control condition. As this technology become increasingly advanced, there is a growing fearfulness that they may surpass human intelligence service and control condition. This fearfulness stems from the thought that once AI has the power to think and make decision on its own, world may no longer be able to exercise authorization over it. This deprivation of control condition raises several ethical question and airs significant hazard to club. One of the main concerns associated with AI's liberty is the passiveness that it may lead to the supplanting of human worker. As AI system become more efficient and capable, they may outperform world in various fields, rendering human labor disused. This can have wide-ranging deduction for the occupation marketplace, leading to unemployment and socio-economic inequality. The deficiency of control condition over AI system may result in their abuse or use, which could have severe consequence for club. If AI system are left unchecked, they may make decision that prioritize their own aim over human wellbeing, leading to potentially harmful result. The number of human control condition becomes even more complex when considering blockchain engineering. While blockchain is designed to be decentralized and transparent, it raises question about who retains control condition on the web. As blockchain system become more prevalent, they may challenge traditional institution such as Banks and government, thereby redistributing powerless. While this decentralization may be beneficial in some aspect, it also raises concern about answerability and regulatory inadvertence. Without centralized control condition, it becomes challenging to hold person or entity accountable for their action, which may lead to illegal or unethical activity. Thus, although blockchain engineering has the potential to enhance transparency and protection, it also poses hazard by shifting control away from established government. With the coming of quantum computer science, the inquiry of control condition becomes even more pertinent. Quantum computer have the potential to process info at unprecedented speed, surpassing the capability of classical computer. This velocity also raises concern about the power to control and predict the result of quantum calculation. Unlike classical computer, quantum system are governed by probabilistic principle, making it difficult to ascertain the exact result of a calculation. This uncertainties introduces a new degree of capriciousness, challenging human control condition over the engineering. The immense powerless of quantum computer also poses a potential menace to cryptographic system, which rely on the computational trouble of certain problem to ensure protection. If quantum computer become powerful enough to break this cryptographic system, it may compromise the unity of information and communicating, making it difficult to maintain control condition and protection over sensitive info. To address these concern, it is crucial to establish model and regulation that ensure human control condition and answerability in the evolution and execution of this technology. This requires coaction between government, manufacture leadership, and academic institution to develop ethical guideline and standard. Transparency and public battle are key in maintaining human control condition. By involving various stakeholders, including the populace, in the decision-making procedure, we can ensure that the evolution and deployment of AI, blockchain, and quantum computing technology align with human value and interest. In decision, the number of liberty and human control condition poses significant challenge and hazard as artificial intelligence service, blockchain engineering, and quantum computing go on to advance. The potential supplanting of human worker, the redistribution of powerless with blockchain engineering, and the uncertainties and potential menace posed by quantum computing all raise ethical concern. It is imperative that we establish regulatory model and prosecute in multidisciplinary discussion to ensure that this technology are developed and utilized in a manner that prioritizes human control condition and answerability. By doing so, we can harness the benefit of this technology while mitigating their potential hazard. The outgrowth and rapid evolution of artificial intelligence service, blockchain, and quantum computing have brought about significant change and break in various industry and fields. This transformative technology have the potential to revolutionize the manner we live, piece of work, and interact with each other, creating both tremendous opportunity and fundamental challenge. Artificial AI mention to machine or system that can simulate human intelligence service and perform undertaking that would typically require human intelligence service, such as address acknowledgment, decision-making, and problem-solving. Over the past secondary, AI has made remarkable advancement, thanks to promotion in simple machine acquisition and deep acquisition algorithm, as well as the handiness of vast sum of information and computing powerless. AI-powered system have been increasingly deployed across numerous sector, including health care, finance, transportation system, and amusement, with the purpose of enhancing efficiency, productiveness, and user see. For case, AI algorithm can analyze medical image to aid in the diagnosing of disease, predict inventory marketplace tendency, and recommend personalized amusement message based on person preference and behavior. Blockchain, on the other minus, is a decentralized and distributed digital Leger that allows for procure and transparent minutes and interaction without the demand for mediator. Originally developed as the engineering underpinning the cryptocurrency Bitcoin, blockchain has gained significant attending and acceptance beyond the kingdom of digital currency. Its alone property, such as immutableness, transparency, and decentralization, make it suitable for application in various spheres, including provision concatenation direction, finance, health care, and administration. For case, blockchain can enable the traceability and transparency of merchandise throughout the provision concatenation, facilitate procure and efficient cross-border payment, and enhance the privateers and protection of electronic wellness record. Quantum computer science, a battlefield that focuses on harnessing the principle of quantum mechanism to build powerful computer, holds the hope of solving complex problem that are currently intractable for classical computer. Compared to classical spot, which can represent either a 0 or 1, quantum spot or qubits can simultaneously represent 0 and 1 due to quantum principle of superposition and web. These belonging enables quantum computer to perform certain calculation exponentially faster than classical computer, potentially revolutionizing fields such as optimization, cryptanalysis, and dose find. Quantum computer science is still in its early phase, and significant technical and technology challenge need to be overcome before it becomes commercially viable. Despite the distinctive feature and application of this three technology, they are not mutually exclusive, and there are potential synergy among them. For illustration, AI can leverage the powerless of quantum computing to speed up complex calculation and enable the preparation of more exact and robust AI model. In bend, blockchain can provide the necessary substructure to ensure the equity, transparency, and protection of AI system, as well as enable the monetization and communion of AI-generated penetration and model. Conversely, quantum computing can contribute to enhancing the protection and privateers of blockchain system by breaking traditional cryptographic protocol and enabling the designing of quantum-resistant algorithm and protocol. The combining of AI, blockchain, and quantum computing can potentially give ascent to novel application and system that were previously unimaginable, leading to new concern model and societal deduction. Despite the transformative potentiality of this technology, they also raise significant societal, ethical, and legal concern. The proliferation of AI raises question regarding information privateers, algorithmic prejudice, answerability, and occupation supplanting. Similarly, the acceptance of blockchain raise challenge related to scalability, interoperability, free energy ingestion, and administration. The coming of quantum computing raises fear about the potentiality for quantum attack on current cryptographic system and the deduction for cybersecurity. It is crucial for policymakers, research worker, and manufacture stakeholder to collaboratively address these challenge and develop appropriate model, regulation, and best practice to ensure the responsible and ethical evolution and deployment of AI, blockchain, and quantum computer science. In decision, the outgrowth and promotion of artificial intelligence service, blockchain, and quantum computing have the potential to reshape our club, economic system, and lives in profound slipway. This technology enable us to tackle complex problem, enhance our decision-making capability, and create new opportunity for invention and evolution. They also raise significant challenge and hazard that need to be carefully addressed. By embracing this technology while simultaneously addressing their potential negative consequence, we can harness their full potentiality for the improvement of humanness.

VII. CONCLUSION

In decision, the convergence of AI, blockchain, and quantum computing holds tremendous potentiality for revolutionizing various sectors of club. AI, with its power to process immense sum of information, learn from form, and make autonomous decision, is already making significant pace in fields such as health care, finance, and transportation system. The integrating of blockchain engineering, with its accent on transparency, protection, and decentralized peer-to-peer network, has the potential to address some of the inherent challenge in AI, such as the deficiency of reliance and explain ability. The coming of quantum computer science has the potential to exponentially accelerate AI capability, as quantum computer can solve complex problem at an unprecedented velocity. Quantum simple machine acquisition algorithm are being developed to harness the powerless of quantum computer science and heighten AI capabilities further. Despite the immense promise of this convergence, there are several challenge and consideration that need to be addressed. Firstly, there are ethical concern surrounding the usage of AI in various application. Issue such as privateers, prejudice, and answerability need to be carefully addressed to ensure that AI is used for the welfare of club and does not cause injury. Regulation and guideline must be put in topographic point to govern the evolution and deployment of AI system, ensuring that they are transparent, accountable, and aligned with ethical standard. Secondly, the integrating of blockchain and AI presents its own exercise set of challenge. While blockchain engineering addresses some of the reliance and protection issue in AI system, it also introduces scalability and computational challenge. Blockchain network are currently incapable of handling the immense computational demand of AI algorithm, and inquiry is required to develop efficient and secure solution. The integrating of blockchain and AI requires careful circumstance of information privateers. The decentralized nature of blockchain may conflict with certain privateers regulation, and mechanism must be put in topographic point to reconcile this issue. The integrating of quantum computer science and AI present both opportunity and challenge. Quantum computer science has the potential to exponentially enhance AI capability by enabling the process of vast sum of information simultaneously. Quantum algorithm for simple machine acquisition are still in their babyhood, and significant inquiry and evolution are required to fully harness the powerless of quantum computing in AI application. Quantum computing introduce protection concern, as it has the potential to break conventional encoding algorithm. New encoding technique and protocol need to be developed to ensure the protection and privateers of information in quantum AI system. In summary, the convergence of artificial intelligence service, blockchain, and quantum computer science has the potential to reshape various aspects of club. AI's power to process information and make autonomous decision, combined with the transparency and protection of blockchain, and the exponential process powerless of quantum computer science, can open up new frontier in health care, finance, transportation system, and other sector. Challenge and consideration such as ethical concern, scalability, computational demand, information privateers, and protection need to be carefully addressed to ensure the responsible and beneficial integrating of this technology. Collaboration between research worker, policymakers, and manufacture stakeholder is crucial to advancing the evolution and deployment of AI, blockchain, and quantum computer science, towards a hereafter that harnesses their full potentiality while ensuring the wellbeing and successfulness of club.

RECAP OF THE MAIN POINTS DISCUSSED

In this try, we have explored the fascinating fields of artificial intelligence service, blockchain, and quantum computer science. We began by providing an overview of this technology and their potential wallop on various industry. We discussed how artificial intelligence service is revolutionizing the manner we work, live, and pass on. From autonomous vehicle to virtual assistant, AI has the powerless to transform our life in slipway we never thought possible. We also highlighted the ethical deduction associated with AI, such as privateers concern and the supplanting of certain occupation. Moving on to blockchain, we delved into the decentralized nature of this engineering and its power to bring transparency and protection to various industry, including finance and provision concatenation direction. We discussed the conception of a distributed Leger and how it can mitigate fraudulent activity by providing an immutable phonograph record of minutes. We examined the function of cryptocurrencies in the blockchain ecosystem, focusing on the revolutionary potentiality of digital currency like Bitcoin and their power to disrupt traditional bank system. We explored the enigmatic universe of quantum computer science. We discussed the principle of quantum mechanism and how they are leveraged to create powerful computational system. Quantum computer have the potential to solve complex problem that are currently beyond the capability of classical computer. From dose find to optimization algorithm, the possibility is endless. We also acknowledged the challenge associated with edifice practical quantum computer, such as the sensitiveness to environmental factor and the demand for mistake rectification. Throughout our treatment, we emphasized the interconnection of this technology and how they can work in bicycle-built-for-two to push the boundary of invention. For case, the immense computational powerless of quantum computer can enhance the capability of AI algorithm, allowing for more sophisticated information analytic thinking and anticipation. Blockchain engineering can provide the necessary protection and reliance for AI system by ensuring the unity and privateers of information. We also highlighted the potential hazard and concern associated with this technology. For case, the rapid promotion of AI raises question about the hereafter of piece of work and the supplanting of occupation. With algorithms becoming increasingly sophisticated, there is a growing care that certain occupation could become obsolete. The aggregation and usage of personal information in AI system raise ethical concern regarding privateers and accept. In the linguistic context of blockchain, there are concern surrounding the free energy ingestion associated with excavation cryptocurrencies. The energy-intensive nature of the procedure has drawn unfavorable judgment due to its C footmark. The decentralized nature of blockchain can also create challenge related to administration and ordinance, as it is inherently resistant to centralized control condition. We discussed the potential wallop of quantum computing on encoding and cybersecurity. While quantum computer have the potential to break existing encoding algorithm, they also offer the chance to develop quantum-resistant cryptanalysis. Thus, research worker and expert in the battlefield are working tirelessly to develop new cryptographic technique that can withstand the powerless of quantum computer. In decision, artificial intelligence service, blockchain, and quantum computer science are shaping the hereafter of engineering and have the potentiality to transform various industry. From AI-enabled personal assistant to transparent and secure blockchain network, this technology offer unprecedented opportunity for invention and promotion. It is crucial to consider the ethical deduction, hazard, and challenge associated with their deployment. As we navigate the ever-evolving landscape painting of engineering, it becomes imperative to strike a proportion between advancement and duty. By understanding and addressing these concern, we can fully harness the powerless of AI, blockchain, and quantum computing while ensuring a safe and equitable hereafter for all.

IMPORTANCE OF CONTINUED RESEARCH AND DEVELOPMENT

In the fields of AI, blockchain, and quantum computer science is of utmost grandness in order of magnitude to harness the full potentiality of this technology and address their inherent restriction. The rapid gait of technological promotion calls for a continuous committees to inquiry and evolution to not only deepen our apprehension of this technology but also identify new application and capability that can benefit club as a unit. Firstly, in the battlefield of AI, continued inquiry is necessary to overcome the restriction that currently hinder its widespread acceptance. Despite the significant advancement made in AI, there are still challenges that demand to be addressed. For case, AI system often lack the power to ground, explain their decision, and understand linguistic context. By investing in inquiry and evolution in AI, we can strive to make this system more explainable, robust, and trusty. This will not only enhance their application in various industry such as health care and finance but also ensure that these AI system are accountable, translating into increased reliance from the general populace. Inquiry and evolution in AI can enable the evolution of novel algorithm and technique that push the boundary of what is currently achievable. As the requirement for AI application turn, so does the demand for more sophisticated algorithm and approach. This requires continuous inquiry in area such as deep acquisition, support acquisition, and natural linguistic communication process.

By continually refining and improving this algorithm, we can enhance their efficiency and truth, opening up new possibility for AI in area as diverse as autonomous vehicle, personalized medical specialty, and clime alteration anticipation. Similarly, continued inquiry and evolution in blockchain engineering are imperative to fully understand its potential and address its restriction. Blockchain has gained attending for its power to provide procure and transparent minutes, especially in the financial sphere. There are still concern surrounding scalability, free energy ingestion, and regulatory challenge. By investing in inquiry and evolution, we can explore novel consensus mechanism, scalability solution, and privacy-preserving technique that can address these restriction and make blockchain engineering more practical and accessible. Inquiry and evolution in blockchain can lead to the evolution of new application beyond the kingdom of finance. For case, blockchain has the potential to revolutionize provision concatenation direction by providing end-to-end transparency and traceability. By further exploring the potentiality of blockchain in various industry such as health care, free energy, and logistics, we can leverage its benefit to improve efficiency, reduce imposter, and enhance reliance in this sector. Inquiry in blockchain can also contribute to the evolution of interoperability standard, enabling different blockchain network to seamlessly pass on with each other, thereby unlocking the full potentiality of decentralized application and fostering coaction across industry. Continued inquiry in quantum computer science is crucial to unlock its immense computational powerless and revolutionize various fields. Quantum computer have the potential to solve complex problem that are currently intractable for

262

classical computer. The evolution of practical quantum computer is still in its babyhood, with significant technical challenge yet to be overcome. Investing in inquiry and evolution is essential to develop new qubit architecture, mistake rectification technique, and quantum algorithm. By doing so, we can improve the staleness and dependability of quantum computer, paving the manner for discovery in area such as dose find, optimization problem, and encoding. Inquiry in quantum technology can also explore the possibility of quantum communicating and quantum cryptanalysis, which have the potential to provide procure and unhackable communicating channel. This could have profound deduction for industry such as cybersecurity, financial minutes, and authorities communicating, creating new opportunity and precaution in an increasingly interconnected universe. In decision, continued inquiry and evolution in the fields of artificial intelligence service, blockchain, and quantum computer science are necessary to fully harness the potentiality of this technology and address their restriction. By investing in inquiry, we can enhance the capability of AI system, make blockchain more practical and accessible, and unlock the immense computational powerless of quantum computer. This inquiry can lead to new application and possibility across various industry, improving efficiency, transparency, and protection. As engineering continues to evolve, the grandness of continued inquiry and evolution cannot be understated in shaping the hereafter of this transformative technology.

POTENTIAL FOR TRANSFORMATIVE EFFECTS ON VARIOUS INDUSTRIES

Potential for transformative personal effects on various industry AI, blockchain engineering, and quantum computing have emerged as powerful tool that have the potentiality to transform various industry. This technology are poised to revolutionize the manner we work, pass on, and behavior concern, offering unprecedented opportunity and creating new challenge. AI has already started making wave in industry such as health care, finance, and fabrication. Its power to perform complex undertaking with velocity, truth, and efficiency has the potential to enhance productiveness and streamline trading operations. For case, in health care, AI-powered algorithm can analyze vast sum of medical information to diagnose disease, place form, and recommend personalized intervention plan. This not only improves patient result but also reduces the workload of health care professional, enabling them to focus on more critical undertaking. Similarly, in finance, AI can automate routine procedure such as client religious service, imposter sensing, and hazard appraisal, enabling financial institution to operate more efficiently and securely. In fabrication, AI-powered automaton and machine can automate product line, reducing cost, increasing productiveness, and improving merchandise caliber. These just scratch the Earth's surface of the transformative potentiality of AI, and as the engineering continues to advance, its wallop on various industry will only grow. Blockchain engineering, often associated with cryptocurrencies like Bitcoin, has the potential to revolutionize industry beyond finance. It offers a decentralized and transparent record-keeping scheme, where minutes are permanently recorded on a distributed Leger. This eliminates the demand for mediator, reduce cost, and provides greater protection and reliance. In industry such as provision concatenation direction, blockchain can enable end-to-end nimbleness and traceability, ensuring the genuineness of merchandise and reducing forge. It can also bring transparency to area like voting system, reducing imposter and enhancing democratic procedure. Blockchain-enabled smart contract can automate the executing of agreement, reducing the demand for mediator and ensuring the enforcement of footing. This has application in fields such as real land, intellectual belongings, and provision concatenation logistics. As blockchain engineering continues to evolve and mature, its potential for transformative personal effects on various industry become increasingly evident. Quantum computer science, still in its babyhood, holds the hope of solving complex problem at an unprecedented velocity. Unlike classical computer science, which uses spot to represent info as either a 0 or 1, quantum computer use quantum spot AI qubits), which can represent info as both 0 and 1 simultaneously. This enables quantum computer to process vast sum of information in analogue, potentially solving problem that are currently beyond the capability of classical computer. One country where quantum computer science has tremendous potentiality is in cryptanalysis. The powerless of quantum computer science could render traditional cryptographic algorithm disused, necessitating the evolution of new encoding method that can withstand quantum attack. Industry that heavily rely on optimization, such as logistics and financial portfolio direction, could benefit from the power of quantum computer to quickly analyze large datasets and find optimal solution. Quantum computer science has the potential to accelerate dose find, molecular mold, and material designing by simulating complex system and interaction. Although still in its early phase, quantum computing holds immense hope and could revolutionize numerous industry in the hereafter. While AI, blockchain, and quantum computing offering significant trans-formative potentiality, they also present challenge that need to be addressed. Ethical consideration surrounding AI, such as prej-udice in algorithm or the potential for occupation supplanting, need to be carefully managed. The protection and privateers deduction of blockchain demand to be fully understood and mit-igated to avoid vulnerability. Quantum computing airs challenge in footing of scalability, mistake rectification, and ensuring the staleness of qubits. Addressing these challenge requires inter-disciplinary coaction between research worker, policymakers, and manufacture leadership to develop robust model, regula-tion, and guideline. In decision, AI, blockchain, and quantum computing have the potential to bring about transformative per-sonal effects on various industry. From improving health care result through AI-powered diagnosis to revolutionizing provision concatenation direction through blockchain-enabled transpar-ency and traceability, this technology offer unprecedented op-portunity for invention. Quantum computer science, while still in its early phase, holds hope in solving previously unsolvable problem and transforming industry such as cryptanalysis and optimization. To fully harness the potentiality of this technology and mitigate associated challenge, it is essential for stakeholder to collaborate and develop ethical model, regulation, and guideline that strike a proportion between invention and responsible usage. As industry continue to embrace this technology, we are likely to witness a prototype displacement that will shape the hereafter of piece of work, communicating, and concern. Final thoughts on the intersection of AI, blockchain, and quantum computing. In decision, the intersection point of AI, blockchain, and quantum computing present a battalion of opportunity and challenge for various sector and industry. The convergence of this technology has the potential to revolutionize the manner we live, piece of work, and interact with the surrounding universe. It is important to carefully consider the deduction and ethical consideration that come along with this promotion. First and foremost, the combining of AI and blockchain has the paleness to enhance and improve the technology we use nowadays. As AI continues to evolve and become more sophisticated, it can be utilized to process and analyze vast sum of information stored on the blockchain. This can lead to more accurate and efficient decision-making procedure, improved protection, and increased transparency in various sectors such as health care, finance, and provision concatenation direction. The integrating of AI and blockchain can help address some of the existing challenge and concern associated with this technology. For case, AI algorithm can be used to detect and prevent fraudulent activity within the blockchain web, ensuring the unity and rustiness of the information stored on it. The usage of decentralized AI model can address the number of information privateers by allowing person to retain control condition over their personal info while still benefiting from AI application. The combining of AI and blockchain can pave the manner for the evolution of autonomous and decentralized system. With AI-powered smart contract and decentralized autonomous organization AI DAOs), it is possible to create self-executing contract and organization that operate autonomously without the demand for mediator or centralized control condition. This can lead to greater efficiency, transparency, and reliance in various sectors such as administration, finance, and provision concatenation direction. On the other minus, the integrating of quantum computing with AI and blockchain introduce a whole new degree of complexes and potentiality. Quantum computer science has the potential to exponentially increase computational powerless, allowing for the process and analytic thinking of complex problem that are currently infeasible for classical computer. This can greatly enhance the capability of AI system by enabling faster preparation and relation, as well as solving optimization problem more efficiently. The usage of quantum computing also poses significant challenge and hazard. One of the main concern is the potential menace to the protection of blockchain network. Quantum computer have the power to break the cryptographic algorithm used to secure blockchain minutes, potentially compromising the unity and confidentiality of the information stored on the blockchain. It is crucial to develop and deploy post-quantum cryptanalysis method to safeguard blockchain network from quantum attack. The integrating of quantum computing with AI raises ethical concern related to information privateers and equity. The enhanced computational powerless of quantum computer can lead to the origin of sensitive info from large datasets, raising question about the protective covering of person privateers. The usage of AI algorithm trained on quantum computer can lead to bias and favoritism, as quantum information set may contain inherent bias that are difficult to detect and address. In decision, the intersection point of AI, blockchain, and quantum computing holds great hope for the hereafter. The combining of this technology can lead to innovative solution, increased efficiency, and improved decision-making procedure in various sector and industry. It is important to approach this promotion with cautiousness and address the ethical concern and challenge that arise along with them. By doing so, we can harness the full potentiality of this technology while ensuring their responsible and ethical usage for the improvement of club.

BIBLIOGRAPHY

Boaz Barak. 'Computational Complexity. A Modern Approach, Sanjeev Arora, Cambridge University Press, 4/20/2009

Brierley Price Prior Ltd. 'Syllabus. Regulatory framework of accounting. Level 2, Brierley Price Prior, 1/1/1982

American Nurses Association. 'Code of Ethics for Nurses with Interpretive Statements. Nursesbooks.org, 1/1/2001

Harvey E White. 'The State of Public Administration. Issues, Challenges and Opportunities, Donald C Menzel, Routledge, 1/28/2015

Rick Ng. 'Drugs. From Discovery to Approval, John Wiley & Sons, 6/22/2015

Martin Kleppmann. 'Designing Data-Intensive Applications. The Big Ideas Behind Reliable, Scalable, and Maintainable Systems, "O'Reilly Media, Inc.", 3/16/2017

Martin Christopher. 'Logistics and Supply Chain Management. Pearson, 1/1/2023

T. J. Richmond. 'Cryptocurrency. 3 Books in 1 - The New Ultimate Blueprint To Making Money With Bitcoin, Cryptocurrencies and Understanding Blockchain Technology, CreateSpace Independent Publishing Platform, 12/19/2017

Robert Muchamore. 'Maximum Security. Simon and Schuster, 4/24/2012

Tiana Laurence. 'Blockchain For Dummies. John Wiley & Sons, 4/3/2019

Tiana Laurence. 'Introduction to Blockchain Technology. The many faces of blockchain technology in the 21st century, Van Haren, 1/1/2019

Dimitris N. Christodoulakis. 'Natural Language Processing - NLP 2000. Second International Conference Patras, Greece, June 2-4, 2000 Proceedings, Springer, 6/26/2003

Saxena, Arti. 'Deep Natural Language Processing and AI Applications for Industry 5.0. Tanwar, Poonam, IGI Global, 6/25/2021

Nelson Lasson. 'The History And Development Of The Fourth Amendment To The United States Constitution. Da Capo Press, 1/21/1970

Wolfgang Ertel. 'Introduction to AI. Springer, 1/18/2018

Felix Weber. 'AI for Business Analytics. Algorithms, Platforms and Application Scenarios, Springer Fachmedien Wiesbaden, 3/2/2023

Marjorie Grene. 'The Anatomy of Knowledge. Papers Presented to the Study Group on Foundations of Cultural Unity, Bowdoin College, 1965 and 1966, Routledge & K. Paul, 1/1/1969

Allam Hamdan. 'The Importance of New Technologies and Entrepreneurship in Business Development: In The Context of Economic Diversity in Developing Countries. The Impact of New Technologies and Entrepreneurship on Business Development, Bahaaeddin Alareeni, Springer Nature, 3/12/2021

National Academy of Engineering. 'Frontiers of Engineering. Reports on Leading-Edge Engineering from the 2018 Symposium, National Academies Press, 2/28/2019

N. Gayathri. 'Blockchain, Big Data and Machine Learning. Trends and Applications, Neeraj Kumar, CRC Press, 9/24/2020

Christoph Lütge. 'An Introduction to Ethics in Robotics and AI. Christoph Bartneck, Springer Nature, 8/11/2020

www.ingramcontent.com/pod-product-compliance
Lightning Source LLC
LaVergne TN
LVHW051223050326
832903LV00028B/2234